麦格希 中英双语阅读文库

危险的职业

【美】比林斯 (Billings, H.)　【美】比林斯 (Billings, M.) ●主编

麻欣●译

麦格希中英双语阅读文库编委会●编

全国百佳图书出版单位
吉林出版集团股份有限公司

图书在版编目（CIP）数据

危险的职业 / (美) 比林斯 (Billings. H) , (美)
比林斯 (Billings. M) 主编；麦格希中英双语阅读
文库编委会编；麻欣译. -- 2版. -- 长春：吉林出
版集团股份有限公司, 2018.3（2022.1重印）
（麦格希中英双语阅读文库）
ISBN 978-7-5581-4732-6

Ⅰ.①危… Ⅱ.①比… ②比… ③麦… ④麻… Ⅲ.
①英语—汉语—对照读物②故事—作品集—世界—现代
Ⅳ.①H319.4：Ⅰ

中国版本图书馆CIP数据核字(2018)第045918号

危险的职业

编：麦格希中英双语阅读文库编委会
插　　画：齐　航　李延霞
责任编辑：沈丽娟
封面设计：冯冯翼
开　　本：660mm×960mm　1/16
字　　数：237千字
印　　张：10.5
版　　次：2018年3月第2版
印　　次：2022年1月第2次印刷

出　　版：吉林出版集团股份有限公司
发　　行：吉林出版集团外语教育有限公司
地　　址：长春市福祉大路5788号龙腾国际大厦B座7层
电　　话：总编办：0431-81629929
　　　　　发行部：0431-81629927　0431-81629921(Fax)
印　　刷：北京一鑫印务有限责任公司

ISBN 978-7-5581-4732-6　定价：38.00元

前 言 PREFACE

英国思想家培根说过：阅读使人深刻。阅读的真正目的是获取信息，开拓视野和陶冶情操。从语言学习的角度来说，学习语言若没有大量阅读就如隔靴搔痒，因为阅读中的语言是最丰富、最灵活、最具表现力、最符合生活情景的，同时读物中的情节、故事引人入胜，进而能充分调动读者的阅读兴趣，培养读者的文学修养，至此，语言的学习水到渠成。

"麦格希中英双语阅读文库"在世界范围内选材，涉及科普、社会文化、文学名著、传奇故事、成长励志等多个系列，充分满足英语学习者课外阅读之所需，在阅读中学习英语、提高能力。

◎难度适中

本套图书充分照顾读者的英语学习阶段和水平，从读者的阅读兴趣出发，以难易适中的英语语言为立足点，选材精心、编排合理。

◎精品荟萃

本套图书注重经典阅读与实用阅读并举。既包含国内外脍炙人口、耳熟能详的美文，又包含科普、人文、故事、励志类等多学科的精彩文章。

◎功能实用

本套图书充分体现了双语阅读的功能和优势，充分考虑到读者课外阅读的方便，超出核心词表的词汇均出现在使其意义明显的语境之中，并标注释义。

鉴于编者水平有限，凡不周之处，谬误之处，皆欢迎批评教正。

我们真心地希望本套图书承载的文化知识和英语阅读的策略对提高读者的英语著作欣赏水平和英语运用能力有所裨益。

丛书编委会

Contents

1

Fire in Midair

On March 31, 1998, England's Leeds United soccer team lost a match by a score of 3-0. So the players weren't very happy as they rode in the bus to the airport. But soon they weren't thinking about the *defeat* at all. They were thinking about how *grateful* they were to be alive.

The fire–damaged engine can be seen on the plane that was carrying England's Leeds United soccer team when the plane had to make an emergency landing.

空中惊魂

　　从飞机上就可以看到被大火烧毁的引擎。当飞机不得不紧急降落的时候，机上正携带着英格兰利兹联足球俱乐部的队员。

　　1998年3月31日，那一天，英格兰的利兹联队在一场足球比赛中以0:3输掉了比赛，在开往机场的大巴上，球员们一个个都十分沮丧。但是很快，失利的阴影就被抛到九霄云外，因为他们所想的就是感谢上帝，让他们从一次空难中幸免于难。

defeat *n.* 失败　　　　　　　　　　　　　　　　grateful *adj.* 感谢的

The team was 50 minutes late getting to the airport. It was after midnight before everyone was settled into his or her seat. Captain John Hackett and the rest of the flight crew were busy preparing the plane for flight. During this time, one of the passengers thought he smelled airplane fuel. He mentioned it to the person sitting in the seat beside him. No one else seemed to notice anything, however. Finally, at 12:20 A.M., Captain Hackett steered the plane down the runway. In a moment, the 67-foot *turboprop* plane, with 44 people on board, was *airborne*.

The plane climbed quickly. In just a few seconds it was 150 feet off the ground. Its speed was up to 140 miles per hour. Then, without any warning, the right engine caught fire. Before long, it was completely *engulfed* in *flames*.

Captain Hackett did not know about the fire right away. His

当天晚上，球员们到达机场的时候就已经比原定时间晚了50分钟，等到他们各就各位，已经过了午夜。机长约翰·哈克特和其他的机组人员正忙着为起飞作准备。此时，一名乘客闻到了一股飞机燃料的气味，并且告诉了他旁边的另一名乘客，可是其他人并没有感觉到这股味道。终于，在0点20分，哈克特机长在跑道上发动了飞机。片刻之间，这架67英尺高、载着44名乘客的涡轮螺旋桨飞机开始了它的航程。

飞机爬升得很快，只用了几秒钟就升到了150英尺的高空，并且速度达到了每小时140英里。突然，在没有任何征兆和预警的情况下，飞机的右侧引擎着火了。很快，整个引擎就湮没在烟火之中。

一开始，哈克特并不知道飞机出了问题，因为仪器上显示一切正常，当一

---

turboprop *n.* 涡轮螺旋桨发动机
engulf *v.* 吞没

airborne *adj.* 空运的；机载的
flame *n.* 火焰；火舌

instruments did not show any trouble. He found out only when a crew member entered the cabin and told him. Meanwhile, the flight attendants rushed to calm the passengers. They also told them to prepare for a crash landing.

When the passengers saw the flames, they *screamed* in terror.

"Fire!" yelled some. "There's a fire!"

Others hollered, "Stop! Stop!"

But this was a plane, not a car. Captain Hackett couldn't just put on the brakes. Still, Hackett had to find a way to land the plane in a hurry. The flaming right engine could *explode* at any moment.

Hackett knew what he was supposed to do. Safety rules stated clearly what should be done in such an *emergency*. He was supposed to *circle* the runway. Only then could he land. But Hackett didn't think he had enough time to do that. So he tried something

---

名机组人员来到驾驶舱告知的时候，机长才知道飞机出了故障。与此同时，机上乘务人员冲到乘客舱里安抚乘客，并且通知他们作好飞机迫降的准备。

当乘客们看到火焰的时候，他们开始发出恐怖的尖叫声。

"火！" "着火了"，有的乘客大叫道。

其他人有的也狂喊着："停下，快停下！"

可是这是飞机，不是一辆汽车。对于哈克特机长来说，解决的办法也不是仅仅踩刹车那么简单，他必须想办法让飞机紧急着陆，因为冒火的右引擎随时可能爆炸。

机长哈克特很清楚他此时应该做些什么，按照紧急情况下的安全规则要求，他应该架机围绕跑道盘旋数圈，然后再着陆。可是此时的哈克特清楚他没有足够的时间去那样做了。所以，他决定冒一次险。

---

scream *v.* 尖叫；发出刺耳的声音　　　　　explode *v.* 爆炸；爆发

emergency *n.* 紧急情况　　　　　　　　　circle *v.* 盘旋；旋转

bolder.

The runway at the airport was long. Looking down, Hackett saw that the plane was flying over the last part of it. He had to make a split-second decision. Hackett turned the nose of the plane toward the ground. He knew the only chance of anyone surviving this crash was if he could land the plane on whatever bit of runway was left.

Hackett brought the plane down fast. When it landed, it *bounced* hard several times. Then it rolled off the end of the runway, its nose *plowing* into the grass. The plane *skidded* for 100 yards and stopped just before hitting a fence. The plane's nose was buried in the ground and its tail hung in the air.

The passengers were desperate to get off the plane. They knew it might still explode at any time. David O'Leary, the soccer team's assistant manager, was sitting near an exit door. He tried to open it,

---

机长从飞机上看到了下面长长的跑道，而此时的飞机已经快飞到跑道的尽头了，他必须要做出一个瞬间的决定了。哈克特机长把机头转向了地面方向，此时他很清楚，是否能把机上人员从机毁人亡中拯救出来，就看他能不能让飞机落在尽头处哪怕一点点剩下的跑道上。

哈克特机长驾驶飞机迅速下落，就在着陆的时候，飞机重重地弹了几下然后就滑出了跑道。减速的时候它冲出去了100码，就在要撞上跑道围栏的瞬间停了下来，此时的飞机，头扎在草地里，机尾翘在了半空中。

乘客们不顾一切地往外跑，因为他们知道飞机随时有可能爆炸。坐在紧急出口旁边的是利兹联队的助理经理奥莱利，他用尽全身的力气也没有打开身旁的门，门已经粘住了。最后奥莱利费了九牛二虎之力终于用肩膀

---

bolder *adj.* 需冒险的
plow *v.* 破浪前进；开路

bounce *v.* 弹跳
skid *v.* 打滑；侧滑

but it was stuck. O'Leary *rammed* the door with his shoulder. It flew open. Quickly, he helped people off the plane. Meanwhile the crew opened the two other exits. Because of the plane's *awkward* position, some people had to jump a long way to the ground. Some sprang from the wing, others from the tail.

Although it took about 30 seconds to get everyone off the plane safely, it probably seemed like hours. People were *clamoring* to get out, but those near the exits knew they should wait. They wanted to make sure they weren't going to leap into the flames.

After one player watched his teammates jump from the plane, it was his turn. "I thought for a moment I couldn't do it," he said. When he jumped and rolled over, everyone shouted to him to get away from the plane. No one knew whether or not the *aircraft* was going to blow up. "I'm lucky to be alive," he said.

把门撞飞了，然后他帮助乘客迅速撤离，同时，乘务人员也打开了另外两个紧急出口。然而飞机着陆的地点实在太别扭了，逃出来的人只好从高高的机身上跳到地面，有的从机翼上跳，有的则从尾部往下跳。

尽管整个撤离过程只用了三十几秒，逃亡的人却感觉像过了几个小时那么漫长。他们大呼小叫地往外跑。而离门比较近的乘客并不着急往外跑，因为他们害怕会跳到火海里面去。

一名球员眼看着自己的队友们逃离了飞机，轮到他往下跳了。"我犹豫了片刻，我真的有些迈不动步了。"他事后描述道。当他跳下来并且滚到一旁的时候，所有的人都向着他大声叫嚷，让他赶快离飞机远点，因为谁也不知道飞机会不会随时爆炸。他补充说："我真的很幸运，我还活着。"

---

ram *v.* 撞击　　　　　　　　　　awkward *adj.* 不合适的；笨拙的
clamor *v.* 喧嚷　　　　　　　　　aircraft *n.* 飞机

With the plane's right engine still burning, the passengers *scurried* to the airport building. A fire crew, wearing special suits, worked quickly to put out the fire.

Both passengers and crew agreed that Captain Hackett was a hero. He had done the right thing in landing immediately. To circle the airport for a proper landing would have taken 8 or 10 minutes. There was a strong *possibility* that a wing would have caught fire. Or fuel leaking from the engine could have caused another *explosion*. That would have meant certain death for every person on board.

Thanks to the quick thinking of Captain Hackett, everything turned out all right. To Hackett himself, however, it was all in the line of duty. He didn't see himself as a hero. "I think any other pilot would have *reacted* the same way," he said.

当乘客跑向机场大楼的时候，飞机右边的引擎依然在燃烧。这时一队穿着特殊服装的消防员迅速赶来，很快地把火扑灭了。

事后，无论是乘客还是机组人员都承认哈克特机长在最关键的时候做出了最正确的决定，第一时间让飞机着陆。如果真的按照飞机紧急情况安全要求先在机场上空盘旋数圈，然后再找一个合适的着陆地点的话，这个过程需要八到十分钟，而这段时间里，飞机的机翼极有可能着火，或者由于引擎漏油而产生大爆炸，那就意味着没有人能幸免了。

事实证明，哈克特机长的正确决定挽救了全体乘客和机组人员。而对于机长本人而言，他所做的就是在履行自己的职责。他可没有把自己当作英雄，就像他说的："我想换了任何一个其他的飞行员，在那种情况下都会做出同样的反应。"

---

scurry *v.* 急跑
explosion *n.* 爆炸

possibility *n.* 可能发生的事物
react *v.* 使起反应

2

Into the Flames

You don't have to be *crazy*, but it helps. This old joke is often used to *describe* people who do dangerous work. A test pilot would be one example. So, too, would a race car driver. But it is hard to think of a more *hazardous* job than smoke jumping.

A want ad for smoke jumpers

Smoke jumpers fight a fire deep in the forest.

火海余生

空降灭火员正在密林深处和大火进行搏斗。

"你不必疯狂，但有时疯狂又是有用的"。这句旧时的笑谈经常用来描述从事危险工作的人，像飞机的试飞员，或者赛车的车手等。但是它们的危险系数和空降灭火的工作比起来，简直就是小巫见大巫。

一般的空降灭火员招聘广告会这样写道："现招聘若干名能够从事空降

---

crazy　*adj.*　疯狂的　　　　　　　　　　　describe　*v.*　描述；形容
hazardous　*adj.*　有危险的

might read like this. "Wanted: A few brave souls who enjoy jumping out of a plane to reach and put out forest fires. Must be willing to land on a *steep slope* or high up in a tree. *Applicants* must not be afraid of raging fire or *choking* smoke. Must be able to cut trees and dig trenches for hours on end. In fact, must be willing to work for days straight without rest. Must also be able to hike miles through the wilderness while carrying a 100-pound pack. And, oh yes, the pay is lousy."

Jumping out of a plane into a fire has always been risky work. Smoke jumpers knew that. But on August 5, 1949, they learned just how deadly their job could be. At 12:25 that afternoon, a fire broke out about 20 miles north of Helena, Montana. It happened in a place called Mann Gulch. The day was hot, dry, and windy. That meant the

---

扑灭森林大火的消防员。应征者需具备如下条件：有勇敢的精神；能够在陡峭的山坡或者树梢降落；不惧怕猛烈的大火和令人窒息的浓烟；可以连续数小时砍伐树木，挖壕沟；事实上，还要具有数天连续不休息地工作和背负100磅重包裹在野外连续数英里跋涉的能力。当然了，报酬是相当诱人的。"

空降灭火员知道，从飞机上跳入火海永远是一项危险的任务。而在1949年8月5日那一天，他们亲身体会到了他们的工作距离死神是多么的近。当天下午12点25分，大火在蒙大拿州海伦娜市北部20英里处燃起，事发地点是在一个叫作曼恩峡谷的地方，当时天气干旱炎热，而且风力十足，火势很快就要蔓延开来。曼恩峡谷地处荒野深处，近处没有任何道路

---

steep   *adj.* 陡峭的   slope   *n.* 斜坡

applicant   *n.* 申请人；申请者   choke   *v.* 使窒息

fire would *spread* quickly. Mann Gulch was deep in the *wilderness*. It was far from any roads. So this was clearly a job for smoke jumpers.

Fifteen smoke jumpers answered the call. They climbed onto a plane and flew to the gulch. At 3:30 P.M., they *parachuted* into the woods. The jump didn't go well. High winds forced the men to jump higher than they had planned. As a result, they landed far apart. It took them more than an hour to find each other.

Still, that didn't seem like a big deal at the time. The fire looked routine. "I took a look at the fire and decided it wasn't bad. ... I thought it probably wouldn't *burn* much more that night," said one.

Because the fire didn't look bad, the group took their time getting organized. Their leader's name was R. Wagner "Wag" Dodge. As Dodge gathered the men together, he heard someone shouting near

---

可行，很明显，现在需要空降灭火员上阵了。

　　15名空降灭火员接受了此次出征的命令，他们登上飞机来到曼恩峡谷。下午3点30分的时候，他们空降到密林之中。但是降落并不十分理想，大风使得他们的着陆点比原来的目标高了一些，而且队员们降落得七零八落。一个小时后他们才得以重新聚拢到一起。

　　起初，问题看起来并不严重，火势也不猛烈。队员们聚拢以后，他们中的一个人说："我看到大火了，问题不大，我想也许明天早晨之前火就会熄灭的。"

　　因为火势并不严重，灭火队在队长的领导下从容地进行着组织工作。队长的名字叫R. 瓦格纳·道奇，大家都叫他瓦格·道奇。就在道奇队长把队员聚拢到一起的时候，他听到有人在大火附近大声呼叫。呼叫的人是吉

---

spread　v. 伸展；蔓延　　　　　　　　　　wilderness　n. 荒地
parachute　v. 跳伞　　　　　　　　　　　　burn　v. 烧毁；燃烧

the fire. It was Jim Harrison, a forest *ranger*. Harrison had been the first to see the fire. He had been trying to fight it alone for hours. Dodge left the group to speak with Harrison. At 5:40 P.M., he and Harrison rejoined the crew. The men were now ready to put out the fire.

They all headed down the gulch toward the Missouri River. But just then the fire flared up below them. This was no routine fire after all. It was a killer.

Powerful winds fed the flames. These flames leaped as high as 200 feet. *Temperatures* in the blaze *soared* to 1,800 *degrees*. Now the men realized their mistake. They should have put out the fire when they had the chance. But it was too late to worry about that now. The fire was closing in on them. It was moving up the slope at a

---

姆·哈里森，正是这个护林员最先发现的大火，而且他已经独自和大火搏斗几个小时了。道奇让队员原地待命，然后去向哈里森了解情况。下午5点40分，道奇和哈里森回到队伍中，队员们准备去扑灭大火。

队伍沿着峡谷向下朝着密苏里河的方向行进。就在此时，大火在他们的下方猛烈燃烧起来，这根本不是一般的火，它的威力足以要了人的命。

风助火势，火借风威，火舌很快就蹿到了200英尺的高度，其温度足有1800度。现在队员们开始意识到他们犯了错误，本应该早早地就将大火扑灭。但是后悔已经太迟了，大火正以疯狂的速度往上蹿，升向他们所处的斜坡。

---

ranger *n.* 突击队员
soar *v.* 飙升；骤然上升

temperature *n.* 温度
degree *n.* 度

furious speed.

Quickly, Dodge ordered his men to turn around and go back up the gulch. He hoped they could make it up over the *ridge* line and down the other side before the fire overtook them. That seemed to be their only hope. The men dropped their *gear* and ran as fast as they could. It was a race against death. The odds were not good. Forest fires spread faster going up a hill than down. But the men could not run very fast up the steep *incline*.

As they scrambled up the slope, Wag Dodge had another idea. Suddenly he stopped and lit a backfire. This technique was new at the time. The goal was to burn a patch of ground before the main fire could reach it. The fire would move around such a patch because there would be nothing left to burn inside it. By lying down inside the

---

　　道奇立刻命令队员们转身向峡谷上方撤离。他希望队伍能够在大火赶上前尽快地翻过山梁，逃到山的另一侧，看起来这是逃生的唯一希望了。这是一场与死亡的赛跑，队员们丢掉身上的装备，以便能够跑得更快一些。但是，机会并不是均等的——森林大火从下往上烧要比往下烧快得多，而对于队员们来说，沿着陡峭的斜坡往上攀登，速度就更快不起来了。

　　当他们沿着山坡向上攀登的时候，瓦格·道奇有了一个主意，他突然停了下来，并且点起了逆火。在当时，这个方法还没有人用过，它的目的就是在森林大火到达之前，先放火燃烧一块区域，这样的话，大火抵达的时候就会绕道而行——因为逆火区内已经无树可烧了。这样，匍匐在烧过的逆火区内，消防员就会幸免于难。

---

furious　*adj.* 激烈的；狂怒的

gear　*n.* 装置；工具

ridge　*n.* 山脊

incline　*n.* 斜面；斜坡

burned-out area, a firefighter could save his or her life.

As Dodge lit his backfire, he called to the other men. He wanted them to wait with him and join him in the burned-out *patch*. They refused. Perhaps they thought they could outrun the fire. Or perhaps they didn't understand what he was doing. In any case, they left Dodge on his own. He lay down in the patch he had burned. The fire *skipped* right by him, *sparing* his life.

For the others, the fire was less forgiving. The flames picked off the men one by one. Eleven men, including Jim Harrison, died that day in the gulch. Besides Dodge, only two others *survived*. Somehow they managed to run fast enough to escape the flames. Two other men made it out but died from their burns the next day.

The country was shocked and saddened by the deaths of the

道奇一边点火，一边呼唤其他人，他想让队员们和他一起留在燃烧过的区域内。但是队员们拒绝这样做，也许他们觉得自己能逃离火海，或者他们对道奇的方式有些不太放心。总之，他们把道奇扔了下来，他躺在自己放火烧过的逆火区内，大火就在他身旁蹿过去，但是没有伤害到他。

对于其他人，大火就没那么宽容了。火舌一个接一个地吞噬了队员，包括吉姆·哈里森在内共11个人被火魔夺去了生命。除了道奇之外，只有两名队员得以逃生，他们是跑得最快的两个。另外还有两个人虽然从火海中逃了出来，但是由于烧伤过重，第二天还是没能保住性命。

对于这些空降灭火员的牺牲，全国人都感到震惊和悲哀。然而，作为

patch　*n.* 小块土地

spare　*v.* 赦免；饶过；使不受……的伤害

skip　*v.* 跳过；跃过

survive　*v.* 幸免于；从……逃生

smoke jumpers. Some good did come out of the *tragedy*, however. For one thing, it showed how *unpredictable* a fire can be. A tiny blaze can turn into a raging *inferno*. The Mann Gulch fire also proved the wisdom of starting a backfire. That is a standard technique today.

Beyond that, the fire showed that smoke jumpers needed more and better equipment. Wag Dodge's crew had just one two-way radio. It got *smashed* during the jump. So the men had no way to talk to the outside world. Today a smoke jumping crew will carry several radios.

Clothing has also come a long way. In 1949 the men wore jeans and cotton, long-sleeved work shirts. They wore baseball caps. Today all smoke jumpers wear fire-resistant clothes. They wear hard

---

不幸中的万幸，人们也从这次悲剧中吸取了教训：一方面，它使人们意识到火灾具有很大的不可预测性——星星之火也许就会变成熊熊烈焰；另一方面，曼恩峡谷的大火也证明了逆火原理的效果，直到今天逆火法仍然是救火中一项基本措施。

除此之外，此次大火还反映了空降灭火员需要更多、更好的设备。瓦格·道奇的灭火队只有一台双向无线电，而且还在空降中摔碎了，所以当时他们根本无法和外界取得联系。今天的空降灭火员则要配备数台无线电。

队员的衣服也经历了很大的变化。1949年队员们穿的是牛仔服或棉制的长袖工作衫，戴棒球帽。现在，所有的队员都穿着防火服，戴着安全

---

tragedy *n.* 悲剧；灾难　　　　　　unpredictable *adj.* 不可预测的

inferno *n.* 无法控制的大火　　　　smash *v.* 粉碎

hats. Every smoke jumper carries a small rolled-up shelter. It is made from *aluminum* that doesn't burn. This shelter can come in handy if a fire gets too close. A person can open it up and *crawl* inside. Then he or she can wait for the fire to pass by.

Today's smoke jumpers also follow 10 strict rules. Everyone carries a copy of these rules inside his or her hard hat. One rule is to "*establish* lookouts." Another is to "know your safety zones and escape routes."

Still, smoke jumping remains dangerous. It's a job that saves lives, forests, and property. But it's not for everyone. After all, only a few people would fit the *description* in that want ad.

帽。而且每个队员都随身携带着一个小型的，桶状的防护设备，它是用不可燃的铝材制成的。当大火来袭的时候，队员可以打开它然后匍匐在里面，这样就可以避免大火的伤害了。

今天的空降灭火员也要严格遵守十条规定，每个队员都要在安全帽中携带这些安全规定的小册子。其中一条规则是"设立瞭望台"；还有一条规定是"明确安全地带和逃生路线"。

尽管如此，空降灭火员仍然是一项危险的工作。它是一项拯救生命、拯救森林、拯救财产的工作，但是并不是每个人都适合这项工作。毕竟，能满足招聘广告中所讲条件的人员太有限了。

---

aluminum　n. 铝
establish　v. 建立；创办

crawl　v. 爬行；匍匐进行
description　n. 描述；描写

3

Doctors (and Nurses) Without Borders

Mary Lightfine knew the old man was dying. She washed him and gave him some fresh *blankets* to keep him warm. Then she found a *tent* where he could lie down. But there was nothing more she could do. Lightfine felt *terrible* for him. She said, "I kept thinking ... what a *horrible*

Kosovars in a refugee camp in Macedonia wait in line for medical service.

跨国天使

科索沃人在位于马其顿的难民营前排队等候医疗援助。

玛丽·莱特费恩知道老人已经生命垂危了。她帮助老人擦洗了身子并且给了他几条新毯子来御寒，之后又找了一座帐篷让他在里面躺着。莱特费恩能做的只有这么多了，她很为老人担心。她说："我总是在想，死在难民营里面是一件多么恐怖的事情。"

blanket *n.* 毛毯
terrible *adj.* 可怕的；恐怖的

tent *n.* 帐篷
horrible *adj.* 恐怖的

feeling to be dying in a *refugee* camp."

Lightfine was right. It was very sad for the man to die in such *grim* conditions. But it would have been even worse if Lightfine had not been there to help. She was part of a group called Doctors Without Borders. On this day in 1997, she was in a refugee camp in Macedonia. She was there to help war *victims* from nearby Kosovo.

Doctors Without Borders began in the 1970s. It was started by French doctors. They wanted to give medical care to those who needed it most. That included people in remote parts of the world. It included those who lived through natural *disasters*. It also included victims of war. The doctors knew it was risky to go to some of these places. But they believed everyone should have medical care, no matter where they lived.

赖特费恩说得没错，对于这个老头儿来说在这样严酷的条件下死去的确是一件悲哀的事情。但是假如莱特费恩没有出现的话，可能情况会更加糟糕。她是医援无国界组织的一名成员，1997年的一天，她正在位于马其顿的难民营里面，给附近的科索沃难民提供医疗援助。

医援无国界组织创立于20世纪70年代，是一些法国医生发起的。他们的目的是给那些最需要的人提供医疗服务，包括偏远地区的人、遭受自然灾害的人以及那些战争中的受害者。他们知道如果去某些地区，将会遭受到很大的危险，但是他们也相信无论在哪里，每个人都应该得到医疗服务。

By the 1990s Doctors Without Borders had become a worldwide group. It had about 2,000 workers in more than 80 countries. These workers came from 45 different *nations*. They weren't paid for their services. They were *volunteers*. One of the volunteers was Mary Lightfine.

Lightfine had had a quiet childhood. She spent many of her early years on a farm in Ohio. So she knew how to feed hens and clean out *barns*. When she grew up, she wanted more action in her life. So she became an *emergency room* nurse.

For 16 years Lightfine worked in emergency rooms across the United States. By 1992 she felt ready for a change. She still wanted to help the sick and needy. But she wanted to travel more. She wanted to see other countries and learn about other ways of life.

到20世纪90年代，医援无国界已经成为世界性的组织，它拥有来自80多个国家45个不同民族的大约2000名成员。这些成员都是志愿者，他们的工作是没有报酬的，而玛丽·莱特费恩正是他们中的一员。

莱特费恩有一个安静的童年。她大部分童年时光是在俄亥俄州的农场里度过的，因此她懂得如何饲养母鸡和打扫粮仓。长大以后，她想让自己的生活更加丰富多彩，于是就成了一名急诊室的护士。

莱特费恩在美国不同的地方一共做了16年的急诊室护士，1992年的时候，她决定改变一下工作方式。虽说她仍然想要帮助那些病人和穷人，但是她打算去更多的地方。她想去其他的国家，领略不同的生活方式，当一个朋友建议她加入医援无国界的时候，莱特费恩决定试一试。

---

nation *n.* 民族
barn *n.* 谷仓；粮仓

volunteer *n.* 志愿者
emergency room 急诊室

When a friend suggested Doctors Without Borders, Lightfine decided to give it a try.

It was a decision that changed her life. Over the next eight years, Lightfine worked for Doctors Without Borders in 10 different countries. She gave children *vaccines* in Uganda. She handed out food in Sudan. She *stitched* up wounds in Macedonia.

Along the way, Lightfine saw a lot of suffering. On the day she bathed the dying man, she also *comforted* a woman whose home had been *destroyed* by war. She bandaged a child who had been hurt in the fighting. "If I move fast and don't think about it, I'll be able to perform my work," she said.

Sometimes, though, she could barely believe what she saw. She treated one man who had been beaten by enemy soldiers. Said

---

这是一个改变她生活的决定，在此后的八年里，她作为医援无国界的成员为十个不同的国家提供过医疗援助。在乌干达，她为那里的孩子注射过疫苗；在苏丹，她发放过食物；在马其顿，她为伤员缝合过伤口。

在工作中，莱特费恩目睹了许许多多的伤痛。就在她给这位垂死的老人洗浴的这天，她还宽慰着一位在战争中失去家园的老妇人；她还给一个在战争中受伤的孩子包扎伤口。她说："如果我行动迅速并且不去多想的话，我就能够完成自己的任务了。"

虽然这么说，她有时还是无法相信自己所见的一切。她曾经治疗过一名被敌人折磨过的男子，莱特费恩讲述道："从腰部往下，'他'都是像

---

vaccine *n.* 疫苗   stitch *v.* 缝；缝合

comfort *v.* 安慰；鼓舞   destroy *v.* 破坏；毁坏

Lightfine, "From his waist down [he] was blue like a gym bag. He had been *tortured* and beaten. In all the emergencies I have worked, I have never seen any person bruised that much. It was very difficult for me to *imagine* that someone could do that to another person."

It was not just the physical wounds that were hard to look at. Lightfine also saw people in great *emotional* pain. Some had lost their homes. Others had seen family members killed. Many feared their lives would never return to normal. "Sometimes the most important thing I do is to hold their hand," Lightfine said.

With children, Lightfine often gave out markers. She had them draw pictures. She found that was a good way for them to *express* their feelings. Many drew burning houses or soldiers with guns. Some even made drawings of people being killed.

体操袋一样的青色。 在所经历的急诊中，我从来没有见到过这样残忍的折磨和践踏，我怎么也想象不到人怎么会对自己的同类如此的狠毒。"

让莱特费恩触目惊心的不仅仅是肉体上的伤口，还有那些心灵上的创伤。在接受援助的人中，有的失去了家园、有的亲人被杀害、还有许多人害怕他们的生活永远也不会恢复到以前的模样。 "有时候我能做的最重要的事情就是握住他们的手"，莱特费恩讲道。

和孩子们在一起的时候，莱特费恩经常给他们发一些卡片，让他们在上面画画，对于孩子们来说，这是一个表达情感的好办法。她看到许多孩子在卡片中绘画燃烧的房屋或者拿着枪的士兵；一些孩子甚至画上人们正在遭受屠杀的场面。

---

torture *v.* 折磨；拷问
emotional *adj.* 情绪的；感情的

imagine *v.* 想象
express *v.* 表达

On most days Lightfine was at work by 7 A.M.. Often she did not stop until midnight. Even when she did have some free hours, she had no place to relax. Her living space was not exactly *plush*.

In Nicaragua, for instance, Lightfine lived in a tiny house along with several others. "It's very basic," she wrote at the time. "There's no *stove* or refrigerator, and we're eating only canned food. I'm sleeping on a mat on the floor of a windowless *pantry*."

Lightfine went on to describe the heat. She wrote, "It's so hot here that even sleeping with one sheet and a fan on is uncomfortable. I don't have a *thermometer*, but it must be near 100 degrees."

In Sudan things were even worse. Some of the time she lived in a pup tent. The rest of the time she slept in a mud shelter. Lightfine

---

大多数日子里，莱特费恩从早晨7点开始工作，经常是在午夜之后才能休息。即使是有了休息的时间她也没有地方放松一下，因为她的居住空间太局促了。

比如在尼加拉瓜，莱特费恩和另外几个人一起住在一所小房子里。"一切都是最基本的。"当时她写道，"那是一间没有窗户的食品储藏间，我就睡在地板上的席子里。没有炉子，也没有冰箱，我们只能吃罐头食品。"

她接着描述当时的炎热。"这里热得即使只盖一条床单并且上面还吹着风扇，睡觉都不舒服。"她写道，"我没有温度计，但是当时的气温一定是接近100度。"

在苏丹，情况更加糟糕。有时候莱特费恩住在三角形的小露营帐篷里面，其他的时候她就睡在一个泥巴砌成的掩体里。只有她一个人住在掩体

---

plush   *adj.* 豪华的
pantry *n.* 食品储藏室

stove *n.* 火炉
thermometer *n.* 温度计

was the only human in the shelter. But there were plenty of rats to keep her company.

Given the *hardships*, it may seem surprising that Lightfine loved her job. But she did. She liked helping people. Beyond that, she found that the people she treated were always very grateful. Some were so thankful they cried. Others *hugged* her or gave her special blessings. Some tried to share their last *bit* of food with her. In Macedonia one woman threw her arms around Lightfine and kissed her. Said Lightfine,"More people have said thank you here than in 10 years of working in an emergency room back home. When people say thank you, you've made a difference. For me, that is the greatest *gift*."

里，但却有许许多多的老鼠和她做伴。

由于条件极其艰苦，人们也许对她依然热爱自己的工作感到吃惊。但是她的确是这样，她喜欢帮助别人。而且她发现接受过她治疗的人总是对她充满了感激之情。有一些人感动得痛哭流涕；有些人拥抱她，给她以特别的祝福；有些人则和她一起分享仅有的食物。在马其顿，一个妇女伸胳膊抱住她，亲吻她。莱特费恩说："这里的人们对我说谢谢要比在国内的急诊室里面工作十年更有意义。它意味着你已经做了一件很重要的事情，对于我来说，这是最了不起的礼物。"

hardship *n.* 艰难；艰苦
bit *n.* 一点；少量

hug *v.* 拥抱；紧抱
gift *n.* 礼物；赠品

Bass Reeves: Hero of the Wild West

If you were an *outlaw* in the Old West, you knew one thing for sure. You didn't want Bass Reeves on your trail. This U.S. deputy *marshal* almost always got his man. From 1875 to 1907 he *tracked* down outlaws in what is now the state of Oklahoma. During these years, Reeves *captured*

This is Bass Reeves who searched for outlaws in towns such as this one, which is a ghost town today.

荒野英雄

　　这就是巴斯·里弗斯，他曾经追查逃犯的小镇，现在已经成为废墟。

　　如果你是美国西部荒野中逃犯的话，有一件事情对你来说是确定无疑的，那就是你不想让巴斯·里弗斯追查到你的踪迹。这个美国的代理警长几乎总能够擒获他想捉拿的人。从1875年到1907年，他在现在的俄克拉荷马州的这块土地上追捕逃犯，共捕获了3000多名犯罪分子。巴斯·里弗斯是那个年代西部荒野中最出色的警官之一。

---

outlaw　*n.* 歹徒；罪犯
track　*v.* 跟踪；追踪

marshal　*n.* 元帅；司令；最高指挥官
capture　*v.* 俘获；捕获

more than 3,000 *criminals*. Bass Reeves was one of the best lawmen in the Wild West.

No one could have *predicted* such a future for Reeves. He was born a *slave* in 1838. He grew into a tall, strong adult. One day in the early 1860s, he quarreled with his master. A fight broke out between them. Reeves hit his master and knocked him out. Under slave laws, that was a major crime. Reeves knew he could be put to death for striking a white man. So he fled across the Red River to Oklahoma. He lived with the Indians of that *region* for several years.

In 1865 slavery was abolished. Ten years after that, Reeves became a marshal. He was appointed by Judge Isaac Parker. Parker's court was in Fort Smith, Arkansas. But the judge also ruled over Oklahoma. This was the most lawless part of the Old West. It was so bad that some people said, "There is no God west of Fort

当年没有人能预测到他会有如此杰出的成就。里弗斯1838年出生在一个奴隶的家庭,他长得高大强壮。19世纪60年代早期的一天,他同他的主人发生了争吵,进而双方开始动起手来,里弗斯揍了他的主人并且把他打倒在地。根据奴隶法令,这是一项大罪,里弗斯知道殴打白人要被判死刑,所以他渡过红河逃到了俄克拉荷马,并且与当地的印第安人一起居住了数年。

1865年,奴隶制度被废除,十年以后,巴斯·里弗斯成为一名警官。他是被艾萨克·帕克法官提拔起来的,帕克法官的法庭位于阿肯色的福特史密斯,同时他也管理俄克拉荷马地区。这个地区是整个西部荒野中法律触角触及最少的地方,以至于一些人把这个地区称作"无法无天的福特史密斯。"

criminal *n.* 罪犯　　　　　　　　　　predict *v.* 预报；预言
slave *n.* 奴隶　　　　　　　　　　　region *n.* 地区；区域

Smith."

Parker knew how wild the region was. All kinds of outlaws hid out there. Among them were train *robbers*, horse thieves, and killers. Parker wanted these outlaws brought to justice. So he appointed 200 marshals to track them down. One of these marshals was Bass Reeves.

Reeves got the job in part because he knew the region well. He knew where the best *hideouts* were. He knew the likely escape routes. Also, he could speak the languages of the local Indians. So he could turn to them for help when he needed it. *In addition*, Reeves was good with a gun. He was so good, in fact, that his friends wouldn't let him join their shooting contests because they knew he would always win.

Still, being a marshal was a *risky* job. Many outlaws were ready

---

帕克深知这里有多么野蛮。形形色色的逃犯都藏匿与此，他们中有火车抢劫犯、马贼，还有杀手。帕克想要把这些作奸犯科者绳之以法，所以他委任了200名警官来追捕这些逃犯，巴斯·里弗斯正是这些警官中的一员。

里弗斯能得到这份工作一方面是因为他对这个地区十分了解——他知道哪里是最好的藏匿地点，哪一条是最有可能的逃生路线；另一方面，他会说当地印第安人的语言，因此必要的时候他可以求助印第安人的援助。除此之外，里弗斯还有一手好枪法。事实上，他的枪法神准以至于同伴们都不让他参加他们的射击比赛，因为只要里弗斯参赛，他们就没有得第一的可能了。

尽管如此，作为警长是一项很危险的工作，许多罪犯已经作好决一死战

---

robber   *n.* 强盗；盗贼

in addition   另外；此外

hideout *n.* 隐匿处

risky *adj.* 危险的；冒险的

to fight to the death. Marshals were often killed in shootouts. Others were killed in ambushes. Like all marshals, Bass Reeves was a marked man. Outlaws wanted very much to see him dead. Many times they shot at him. But they always missed. They never even wounded him.

Reeves was, of course, lucky. But he was also very smart. He knew it was safer to *sneak up* on outlaws than make a direct charge at them. And Reeves was a master of disguise. He often posed as a cowboy or farmer. Outlaws often didn't know who he was until he snapped the *handcuffs* on them.

Once Reeves went after two young outlaws near the Texas border. He heard they were hiding at their mother's home. So he decided to pay them a visit. But he didn't go dressed as a U.S. marshal. Instead, he dressed up as a *tramp*. He put on an old *floppy*

的准备。警长们经常死于枪战。另一些则死于伏击。和所有的警长一样，巴斯·里弗斯是引人注目的。歹徒们非常想看到他死，许多次他们向他射击，但是他们总是错过，他们甚至没有使他受伤。

里弗斯当然是幸运的，而他也很聪明——他知道偷偷地跟踪逃犯要比直接向他们发难安全得多。他是一个伪装大师，经常把自己装扮成一个牛仔或者农夫，经常是逃犯还没有弄清他是谁就已经被咔吧一声铐上了手铐。

有一次里弗斯在得克萨斯边界附近追逐两个年轻的逃犯。他听说逃犯将要躲藏到他们母亲的家里，于是决定去那里拜访。但是他没有穿着联邦警员的制服出发，取而代之的是把自己扮成了一名流浪汉。他戴着一顶邋遢的帽子，为了让别人不怀疑他的身份，里弗斯还在帽子上射了三个洞。

---

sneak up 悄悄地靠近
tramp n. 流浪者

handcuff n. 手铐
floppy adj. 邋遢的

hat. To make it look *authentic*, Reeves *shot* three holes in it. He left his horse at a camp 28 miles away. Then he made the long, hot walk to the mother's house.

By the time he got there, he was tired and dirty. He really did look like a tramp. Reeves knocked on the door. He begged the mother for a bite to eat, telling her how hungry he was. He said his feet hurt from walking so far. He also *mentioned* that marshals were after him and had nearly killed him. He took off his hat and showed her the three bullet holes.

The mother took pity on Reeves. She invited him in. She gave him food and began chatting with him. She told him about her two outlaw sons. She even suggested that he might join them in a life of crime.

Later the mother heard a *whistle*. It came from her sons. They

---

他把自己的马留在了28英里以外的营地，然后就开始了向逃犯母亲家酷热地长途跋涉。

当他到达的时候，已经是疲惫、肮脏不堪了，确实像一个流浪汉。里弗斯敲开了门，向两个逃犯的母亲讨要一口吃的。他对老太太说自己已经是饥饿难当，并且他的脚也由于长途跋涉而受伤。里弗斯还给她看了看帽子上的三个弹孔，然后透露说后面有警察正在追捕他，而且差点要了他的命。

那个母亲很可怜里弗斯，把他让进了屋子，给他拿了些食物然后就和他攀谈起来。她讲述了自己的两个逃犯儿子，甚至鼓励里弗斯也加入他们的犯罪团伙。

随后这位母亲听到了一声口哨。那是她儿子吹的，这两个家伙想知

---

authentic *adj.* 真正的；真实的
mention *v.* 说起；提到

shoot *v.* 射击
whistle *n.* 哨声

had been hiding during the day and wanted to know if it was safe to return home. The mother signaled back that all was clear. When the sons appeared, the mother *introduced* them to Reeves. They agreed to let him join their gang.

With darkness falling, Reeves was invited to spend the night. As soon as the outlaws fell asleep, he handcuffed them to their beds without waking them. In the morning he arrested them. He *marched* them the whole 28 miles back to the camp. For the first three miles the mother followed them, *cursing* Reeves the whole time.

Although Reeves liked to surprise outlaws, he couldn't always do that. So he sometimes squared off against them *face-to-face*. That was the case when Reeves tracked down Jim Webb. Webb was among the worst outlaws in the Wild West. He was a thief and a killer. He had been on the run two years for shooting a black

道家里是否安全。他们已经在外面藏了一天了，此时如果安全他们就要回来。老太太向他们发出信号表示一切都平安无事。当儿子回来的时候，她还把他们介绍给里弗斯，哥俩答应让里弗斯加入他们的团伙。

夜幕降临的时候，哥儿俩邀请里弗斯在他们家里留宿。等到哥俩一睡着，里弗斯就轻手轻脚地把他们铐在了床上，第二天一早逮捕了他们，然后赶着他们返回了28英里以外的营地。在开始往回走的时候，两个逃犯的妈妈一直在后面跟了三里地，不停地咒骂里弗斯。

虽然里弗斯喜欢给这些歹徒以震慑，但并不总是这样做。当与歹徒面对面时，他有时候是出于自卫才反击，跟踪吉姆·韦伯就是这样的情形。韦伯是西部荒蛮地区最臭名昭著的歹徒之一。他是小偷，也是一个杀手，

introduce v. 介绍；引见
curse v. 诅咒；咒骂

march v. 使进行；前进
face-to-face 面对面的

preacher when Bass Reeves finally cornered him. Although they were 500 yards apart, Webb began firing as fast as he could.

Reeves felt bullets whistling past him. One hit his *saddle*. Another cut a button off his coat. A third cut the reins out of his hands. Reeves didn't flinch. As he leaped off his horse, a fourth shot from Webb ripped through his hat. Still, Reeves stayed calm. He pulled out his *rifle* and took careful aim. Then he fired twice. Webb fell dead in his tracks.

Over Reeves's long *career* as a marshal, he killed a total of 14 men. But he fired his gun only in self-defense. Once Reeves was arrested for murder. He had shot and killed an outlaw whom he was trying to arrest. But during the trial he proved the outlaw had fired first. The court found him not guilty.

曾经枪杀过一名黑人传教士，最后里弗斯把他堵在角落的时候，韦伯已经逃亡两年了。但是他并没有束手就擒，尽管相距有500码远，他却以最快的速度向里弗斯开火了。

里弗斯能够感觉到子弹从他的身边呼啸而过。第一颗击中了他的马鞍子；第二颗把他的一颗纽扣打掉；另外一颗子弹把缰绳从他的手上打落。正当他从马上跳下来的时候，第四颗子弹到了，这一次他的帽子被打了个洞。尽管如此，里弗斯并没有惊慌，他拔出枪，冷静地瞄准然后扣动了两次扳机。韦伯倒下了，死在了他逃亡路上。

在作为警长的生涯中，里弗斯一共打死了14个人，但是他每一次开枪都是出于自卫。有一次他因为谋杀被逮捕，原因是在追捕的过程中枪杀了对方。但是在审判的过程中他证明了自己的清白，是那个歹徒率先开的枪，最后，法院当庭宣布里弗斯无罪。

---

preacher *n.* 牧师；传道士

rifle *n.* 步枪

saddle *n.* 鞍；鞍具

career *n.* 事业；职业

Reeves loved the law. One day near the end of his career he showed everyone just how much he loved it. He learned that a new arrest *warrant* had been issued. It was for a man who had shot and killed his wife. But this time the criminal was not a stranger. It was Reeves's own son.

No one expected Reeves to handle the arrest. But he was determined to do his duty. Sadly, he picked up the warrant and went out after his son. Two weeks later, Reeves arrested him. The son was found guilty and was punished with a long jail *sentence.*

In 1907 Bass Reeves turned in his *badge.* He was ready to *retire.* That same year, Oklahoma became a state. The days of the old Wild West were gone. Bass Reeves had helped bring law and order to the region. Three years later, at the age of 72, Bass Reeves died.

里弗斯热爱法律，而且在他即将退休前的某一天，他用行动向每个人表明了他是多么爱它。当时，他得知一条新的逮捕令已经发出，要逮捕的男子枪杀了自己的妻子。这一次的罪犯不是旁人，而是里弗斯的亲生儿子。

人们都不希望里弗斯来执行这次抓捕工作，但是他下定决心来完成这次任务。他悲痛地接过了逮捕令，开始追捕自己的儿子。两周以后，里弗斯逮捕了儿子。最后他的儿子被判有罪，将要在监狱里服刑很长的时间。

1907年，巴斯·里弗斯上缴了他的警官徽章，他准备退休了。同年，俄克拉荷马变成了美国的一个州，美国西部狂野、荒蛮的时代一去不复返了。是巴斯·里弗斯帮助这个地区建立了法律和新的秩序。三年以后，也就是在他72岁那一年，巴斯·里弗斯离开了人世。

---

warrant *n.* 委任状；证明

badge *n.* 徽章

sentence *n.* 判决；宣判

retire *v.* 退休

Avalanche in British Columbia

The *distress* call went out at 10:16 A.M.."*Mayday*! Mayday!" was heard over the radio. "Portal Camp has been wiped out by a snow slide. Require ... all help possible."

One hundred forty men worked and lived at Portal Camp. The camp was part of a copper *mine run* by the

An avalanche similar to this one destroyed Portal Camp.

雪崩地裂

类似的雪崩毁灭了波特尔营地。

"救命！ 救命！"上午10点16分，紧急的求救信号通过无线电传了过来，"波特尔营地已经被雪崩彻底摧毁了，我们需要……紧急援救。"

波特尔营地是格兰达克矿业公司经营的铜矿的一部分，大约有140个人在里面工作并且居住。这个营地位于北不列颠哥伦比亚省的一个偏远地区，即使离最近的城镇斯图尔特，也有30英里远的距离。

---

distress *n.* 危难；不幸
mine *n.* 矿山；矿井

mayday *n.* 求救信号
run *v.* 经营；管理

Granduc Mining Company. It was in a remote part of northern British Columbia. Stewart, the nearest town, was 30 miles away.

The mine had been open only six months. It was built under a snow-covered mountain. Portal Camp was near the *entrance* to the mining *tunnel*. The camp was like a little town. It had a dining hall, offices, and *bunkhouses*. The men who lived in the camp took turns working in the mine.

In some ways, life wasn't so bad for the miners. They got plenty to eat. They kept each other company. During their free hours they could go to the *recreation* hall. Still, they were in a place with terrible weather. This part of Canada had fiercely cold winters. It also got huge amounts of snow. Often more than 60 feet fell in a single season. The record snowfall was more than 90 feet.

这个矿厂位于一座白雪覆盖的山脚下，它才开张六个月。波特尔宿营区就安置在矿井隧道的入口处附近。整个营地就像一个小的镇子，里面有一间餐厅、几间办事处，还有几间工人们居住的简陋的房子，居住在这里的工人们轮流去矿上工作。

从某些方面来看，工人们的日子还算不错。他们有充足的食物；和同事们的交往使得他们并不孤单；闲暇的时候还可以去娱乐场所消遣一下。然而这里的天气十分糟糕，加拿大的这个地区冬天气候是极其恶劣的。这里冬天的降雪量极大，经常一个季节的降雪量就超过60英尺，最大的降雪量曾经超过90英尺。

---

entrance n. 进口；入口
bunkhouse n. 简易宿舍；工房

tunnel n. 隧道；隧洞
recreation n. 娱乐；消遣

In mid-February 1965, 16 feet of snow fell on the camp. That didn't trouble the miners. To them, the snow just seemed like a *nuisance*. In truth, however, all that snow posed a great danger.

Above Portal Camp sat the Leduc Glacier. This frozen mass of ice lay at the top of the mountain. As new snow *piled* up on the glacier's smooth surface, the conditions became perfect for an avalanche. It was just a matter of time.

On February 18 the time came. Tons of snow *slipped* down the face of the *glacier*. There was no warning. The snow came silently, so none of the men had a chance to run away. The lucky miners were the ones in the tunnel. The unlucky ones were at Portal Camp. There the snow blasted all but one building.

Gus Ritchie was one of about 100 men in the mine when the

1965年2月中旬，一场16英尺厚的雪降落到了波特尔营地，但是并没有给矿工们带来太大的不便，因为对于他们来说，雪就像是一个讨厌的家伙而已。可是实际上，这次大雪却给他们带来了极大的危害。

波特尔营地上面是勒达克冰川，这个巨大的冰块就在山的顶部。当新降落的雪堆积到冰川光滑的表面，就为雪崩创造了极好的条件，现在只是时间的问题了。

2月18日那天，雪崩终于发生了。事先没有任何预兆，成吨的雪顺着冰川的表面滑了下来。由于雪来得没有任何动静，所以人们根本没有任何机会逃走。在隧道里面工作的矿工成了幸运儿，而那些留在波特尔营地的人则成了受害者，除了一幢房屋之外，暴雪摧毁了营地上所有的建筑物。

当雪崩来袭的时候，格斯·里奇正在矿井隧道里面工作，同时工作的

---

nuisance *n.* 令人厌烦的人
slip *v.* 滑动；滑行

pile *v.* 堆积；积累
glacier *n.* 冰河；冰川

avalanche hit. "The slide cut off the power," he said. "We *groped* our way through the darkness until we got near the entrance." There they found a pile of snow blocking their way. "We crawled up over the snow and were amazed by what we saw. [There was] no more mechanic shop, no more *garage*, no more coffee shop. Everything was just *chunks* of wood, steel, and tin."

Was anyone alive under all that *rubble*? It didn't seem possible. Then Ritchie heard a faint moan. He and the others started digging as fast as they could for the survivor. They heard another groan a few feet away. They thought they were digging in the wrong place, so they moved to the new spot. Then they heard several more human sounds. "We were all confused," said Ritchie. "There were people buried all over the place." They dug out eight comrades who were

---

还有大约100个工友。"雪崩造成了停电,"格斯·里奇回忆到,"我们在黑暗中一直摸索到隧道的入口处。"他们发现那里有雪堆阻挡住了前行的路。他说:"我们在雪上爬行,然后看到的场景把我们惊呆了。机械车间、车库、咖啡店都不见了,眼前是一堆一堆的木头、钢铁和罐子。"

碎石堆下面还能不能有人活着呢?看起来希望很渺茫了。当时里奇听到了一声微弱的呻吟,于是他和他的同事开始以最快的速度挖掘可能的幸存者。然后在几英尺外的地方他们又听到了一声呻吟,他们觉得挖错地方了,于是就换了一个新地方接着挖,而后他们又听见了几阵声响。"我们都糊涂了,"里奇说,"好像到处都埋着人。"他们一共挖出了8个同

---

grope *v.* 摸索
chunk *n.* 厚块;大块

garage *n.* 车库
rubble *n.* 碎石;瓦砾

hurt but alive.

They also found a dead miner. "It really hurt me when I found my friend Scotty dead," said Ritchie. "He was in a *crouched* position on his hands and knees. [He] must have died that way as he tried to protect himself from the slide."

One survivor at the camp was Frank Sutherland. He was in the kitchen when the snow *struck*. "First thing I knew, the lights went out." he said. "Then the building took off down the slope and slid half a mile. They had to cut me out with a *chain saw*."

Bertram Owen-Jones, a cook, was also in the kitchen. He was holding a knife when everything went black. The snow blew apart the cookhouse. A piece of the wall fell on Owen-Jones. Still, he never let go of the knife. It took him three hours, but he used the knife to

---

事，这些人都受伤了，但是却还活着。

里奇他们也发现了一个死难的矿工。"当我看到我的朋友斯科蒂死去的时候，我真的十分悲痛，"里奇说，"他抱着胳膊和膝盖，（他）一定是为了在雪崩时候保护自己才那样蜷缩着死去的。"

一个名字叫弗兰克·萨瑟兰的幸存者，雪崩来袭的时候他正在厨房里面。"我能记起来的第一件事就是灯突然灭了。"他说，"然后房子就顺着山坡滑出了半英里。他们不得不用一把链锯弄开房子把我救出来。"

厨师伯特伦·欧文·琼斯当时也在厨房里面。周围一片黑暗的时候他正握着一把刀。大雪把厨房冲裂后，一块墙壁压到了欧文·琼斯的身上，而

---

crouch v. 蜷伏
chain n. 链条

strike v. 打；打击
saw n. 锯子

cut himself free. Other men also managed to free themselves.

Meanwhile, *rescuers* were struggling to reach Portal Camp. These rescuers came from both Canada and the United States. They couldn't drive trucks into the mining camp. The 16 feet of new snow *blocked* all the roads. Some took Snow Cats over the mountains. Others came by air.

After several hours, rescuers finally reached the camp. They picked up 17 miners who were in the worst shape and rushed them to safety. But that left more than 120 men still in the camp. Another avalanche could begin at any moment. The rescuers knew they would have to make more trips to Portal Camp to save these men.

By the next day, though, they found it almost impossible to get to the camp. A *blizzard* was raging there. Wind *whipped* the snow in all

---

他也没有松开那把刀。他用刀在雪里面挖了3个小时，最后把自己救了出来。其他人也各自努力使自己逃离了危难。

与此同时，来自加拿大和美国的救援人员正在全力赶往波特尔营地。可是现在他们已经无法把车开到矿工的营地了，新下的16英尺深的积雪封堵住了所有的道路。有人驾着雪猫翻山越岭驶往营地，另外一些人则乘着飞机往这里赶。

数小时以后，救援人员终于抵达了营地。他们找出了情况最糟糕的17名员工并且立刻把这些人送往安全地带。但是营地里还剩下120多名矿工，下一场雪崩随时有可能袭来，所以救援人员明白，他们必须尽可能多地来回几次以便救出所有的人员。

可是到了第二天，他们发现再想到达营地几乎不可能了，强烈的暴风雪拦住了去路。风从各个方向吹打着地上的积雪，几码以外就什么都看不

---

rescuer *n.* 救助者　　　　　　　　　block *v.* 阻止；阻碍
blizzard *n.* 暴风雪；雪暴　　　　　　whip *v.* 鞭打；抽打

directions. No one could see more than a few yards. Still, *helicopter* pilots bravely agreed to fly into the camp. One of these pilots was Kenny Eichner. He wanted to bring in a doctor to treat wounded miners stranded at the camp.

About a mile from Portal Camp, the storm became too *intense.* Eichner had to land his chopper right on top of the glacier. All night he and the doctor huddled inside the helicopter. The next morning Eichner had to chip ice off the *blades* to get going again.

Even after reaching the camp, rescuers were not safe. The *threat* of another avalanche hung over them all the time. Some filled their choppers with surviving miners and flew out again. Others stayed to look for men still trapped in the snow. Hour after hour they dug. They found one dead body after another. In time their hopes of finding

---

到了。即使这样，一些英勇的飞行员仍然决定驾驶直升机进到营地进行营救，其中就包括飞行员肯尼·埃克纳。埃克纳打算带一名医生进入营地去治疗那些束手无策的矿工。

在距离营地一英里的时候暴风雪异常猛烈起来，埃克纳不得不在冰川顶部降落他的直升机，整个晚上，他和医生就蜷缩在飞机里面。第二天早上，埃克纳把冰从飞机的螺旋桨上清理下去，然后他们再次出发了。

即使到达营地以后，救援人员也不安全。下一次雪崩就像悬在头上的剑一样，随时会冲下来。有些飞行员把幸存的矿工装进飞机里，然后冲出了营地。另外的营救者留下来搜寻仍然埋在雪下的工人。他们一个小时接一个小时的挖，不断地找到一具又一具的尸体，这个时候他们感觉找到幸

---

helicopter *n.* 直升机
blade *n.* 叶片；桨片

intense *adj.* 强烈的
threat *n.* 凶兆；恶兆

survivors *faded*.

After 79 hours they found a buried miner who was still alive. He had been trapped under six feet of snow. Helicopters had landed on top of him. At last a *bulldozer* began to clear away the snow above him. That was when rescuers found him. He was *dehydrated*. He had *frostbite*. But at least he was alive.

After a week of hard work, rescuers still had not sifted through all the snow. But they could stay no longer. So much new snow was falling that another avalanche seemed sure to come. Everyone had to get out of Portal Camp. So now the rescuers themselves had to be rescued.

More pilots flew in through the blinding blizzard. These men spotted Portal Camp only because smoke was still rising from the

---

存者的希望逐渐渺茫了。

就在79个小时以后，搜救者在雪下找到了一名仍然活着的矿工。他被埋在了6英尺深的雪里，直升机曾经在他上面降落过。最后当推土机开始清理压在他上面的积雪时，救援者发现了他。这名矿工已经冻伤了，并且已经脱水，但是至少他活了下来。

经过一周的努力工作，救援人员仍然不能彻底地把积雪都筛一遍，但是他们不能再逗留了。大雪不断地飘落下来，新的雪崩看来是不可避免了，所有的人员必须撤离波特尔营地。而现在，救援人员自己都需要援救了。

越来越多的飞行员穿过让人睁不开眼的暴风雪抵达了营地。他们能到达这里仅仅依靠营地废墟中冒出的烟给他们作信号。暴风雪如此猛烈以至

---

fade *v.* 逐渐消失　　　　　　　　　　bulldozer *n.* 推土机
dehydrate *v.* 脱水　　　　　　　　　　frostbite *n.* 冻伤

ruins. The storm was so bad that one plane slid off the runway at Stewart and hit a *snowbank*.

In all, 26 miners died. More would have died if it hadn't been for the skill and *courage* of the rescuers. Portal Camp was never reopened. The risk of more avalanches was just too great. The Granduc Mining Company had learned a harsh lesson. There are some places that should be *disturbed* only by Nature.

于一架飞机冲出了位于斯图尔特的跑道撞到了路边的雪堤上。

一共有26名矿工死于此次雪崩，但是如果不是救援人员的高超技术和过人的勇气的话，伤亡会更加惨重。波特尔营地从那以后再也没有开放过，雪崩的威胁依然存在。格兰达克矿业公司得到了一次惨痛的教训——有些地方人类是不应该涉足的，那里只属于大自然。

snowbank *n.* 雪堤；雪堆　　　　　　　　courage *n.* 勇气；胆量
disturb *v.* 打扰；妨碍

6

The Spy Who Saved Lincoln

"**B**ut why—why do they want to kill me?" asked Abraham Lincoln.

It was February 21, 1861. Allan Pinkerton, head of the Pinkerton National *Detective Agency*, tried to *explain*. He pointed out that many people in the South hated Lincoln. They hated him with a *passion*. To

Abraham Lincoln is sworn in for his second term as president in 1865.

敌后干探

1865年亚伯拉罕·林肯宣誓第二次就职美国总统。

"但是为什么——他们为什么要杀害我？"亚伯拉罕·林肯问道。

1861年2月21日，平克顿全国侦探事务所的负责人艾伦·平克顿正在向林肯作解释。他指出，南方许多人都在憎恨林肯，甚至怒不可遏。对于

detective *n.* 侦探　　　　　　　　agency *n.* 提供专项服务的机构
explain *v.* 说明；解释　　　　　　passion *n.* 激情；热情

them, he was a *symbol* of the end of slavery and the Southern way of life. Some of these people wanted to see Lincoln dead. A few were even willing to give up their own lives to kill him.

Lincoln had been elected president of the United States in 1860. But he had not yet taken the *oath* of office. That would happen on March 4, 1861. If some Southerners had their way, Lincoln would not live to be president. It was Pinkerton's job to see that these angry Southerners did not kill the future president.

Pinkerton knew of the dangers Lincoln faced because he had sent some of his *spies* to Baltimore, Maryland. The spies posed as Lincoln-haters. They went to secret meetings. These meetings were held to see what could be done about Lincoln. It was at these meetings that Pinkerton's spies learned just how strong Southern

---

这些南方人来说，林肯象征着奴隶制度和南部生活方式的终结。他们中的一些人想要看到林肯的死，甚至有些人不惜以命换命。

在1860年，林肯就已经被选为美利坚合众国总统，但是他还没有正式宣誓就职，那要等到1861年3月4日。如果那些南方人的计划得以实施，恐怕林肯就等不到那一天了。平克顿的工作就是确保这些愤怒的南方人无法杀害这位未来的总统。

平克顿已经派出了若干名手下的侦探前往马里兰的巴尔迪摩市打探情况，所以他深知林肯此时所面临的危险。这些特工人员扮作是仇恨林肯的人，参加秘密专门研究如何对付林肯的集会。就是在这些会上，平克顿的特工人员们体会到南方人对林肯的憎恨有多么强烈。

---

symbol *n.* 象征；标志   oath *n.* 誓言；誓约

spy *n.* 间谍；密探

anger really was.

One man felt an especially powerful rage. He was a *barber* named Cypriano Ferrandini. At one of the secret meetings, he called the future president "most *vile* and *repulsive*." The crowd roared in agreement. They raised clenched fists. Next Ferrandini took out a knife and waved it over his head. He shouted, "Lincoln shall never, never be president. My life is of no consequence in a cause like this. I am willing to give it for his."

When Pinkerton's spies reported back to him, Pinkerton could *barely* believe them. Were the Southerners serious? Or were the wild speeches nothing but hot air? Pinkerton felt he had to check it out for himself. So he went to Baltimore. Like his spies, he pretended to hate Lincoln. Before long, he was introduced to Ferrandini. The two

---

　　其中有一个人尤其强烈地表达了对林肯的痛恨。他叫塞浦里亚诺·费兰蒂尼，是一个理发师。在一次秘密会议上，他称这位未来的总统是"最卑鄙无耻的，最令人厌恶的。"人群都举起了紧握的拳头，狂叫附和着。接下来，费兰蒂尼掏出了一把刀在头上挥舞，并且大声喊道："林肯永远、永远也不会成为总统。他如果上台，我的生命也就没有什么意义了，我要和他拼命，不是他死就是我死。"

　　当侦探们把收集到的情报向平克顿汇报的时候，他并不十分确定这些南方人是认真的呢，还是仅仅说大话？平克顿感到不得不亲自出马了，所以他也动身去了巴尔迪摩。和手下的侦探一样，平克顿也装作是一个痛恨林肯的人，很快他就接近了费兰蒂尼，并且和这名理发师进行了交谈。

---

barber *n.* 理发师　　　　　　　　　vile *adj.* 卑鄙的
repulsive *adj.* 可憎的；令人讨厌的　　barely *adv.* 几乎不；简直没有

men began to talk. Pinkerton asked the barber if there was any way to save the South without killing Lincoln. "No," said Ferrandini. "He must die—and die he shall." That *convinced* Pinkerton that the men were serious. They wouldn't blink at killing a man they saw as their enemy.

Lincoln listened closely to Pinkerton's report. Still, he was not sure the *threat* was real. But the very next day, he heard the same story from Frederick Seward, a trusted friend. It didn't seem likely that both Seward and Pinkerton were wrong. So he turned to Allan Pinkerton. "What do you want me to do?" he asked.

Pinkerton knew Lincoln was about to travel from Pennsylvania to Washington, D.C. On his way, he would pass through Baltimore. Pinkerton *feared* this was when the killers would *strike*.

平克顿当时间费兰蒂尼，如果不杀害林肯的话，是否还有其他的办法来拯救南方呢，得到的回答是"没有。"费兰蒂尼说："他必须死，而且一定会死。"现在平克顿相信了，这个人是认真的。尽管南方人把林肯看作敌人并且要杀害他，但平克顿他们却不能熟视无睹。

　　林肯细细地听取了平克顿的汇报，然而他对于这种危险的可靠性还是不太确定。但是就在第二天，他从一位信任的朋友——弗雷德里克·苏华德那里得到了同样的消息，看来苏华德和平克顿不可能同时都错了。所以林肯转过来求助艾伦·平克顿："你觉得我该怎么做呢？"

　　平克顿知道林肯将要从宾夕法尼亚到哥伦比亚特区华盛顿作一次旅行，中途要经过巴尔迪摩。而平克顿所担心的正是在巴尔迪摩，这些南方的杀手将要发动袭击。

---

convince *v.* 使确信；说服　　　　　　threat *n.* 威胁；恐吓
fear *v.* 害怕；为……担心　　　　　　strike *v.* 侵袭

Lincoln was supposed to arrive in Baltimore by train on February 23. Then he would make his way to another railroad station on the other side of town. He would ride a carriage through the streets. That would give people a chance to come out and wave to him. But it would also give an *assassin* the perfect chance to *attack*. In fact, Pinkerton knew, the killers might strike anywhere along the route to Washington. They might blow up a bridge as Lincoln's train crossed it. Or they could attack Lincoln with guns while he was riding in his carriage. Or a single man could sneak up on him with a knife at the train station. Lincoln couldn't count on the police to save him. The head of Baltimore's police force was himself a Lincoln-hater.

Pinkerton thought of all the *options*. Then he decided Lincoln should play it safe. He advised him to change his *schedule*, but keep

林肯应该在2月23号坐火车抵达巴尔迪摩，然后在那旦乘坐一架四轮马车穿过街市赶往城市另一头的火车站。这样很多人就会涌上街头来向他挥手致意，但是这也成了刺客发动袭击的绝佳机会。其实平克顿心里很清楚，在去往华盛顿的路上，刺客随时随地有可能采取行动。他们可以在林肯的火车经过的时候炸毁桥梁；或者在他乘坐马车的时候用手枪射杀他；或者派出一个人偷偷地在火车站接近他，然后用刀刺死他。林肯认为当地的警察不可能来救助他，因为巴尔迪摩警察部门的头儿也是一个对他怀恨在心的人。

平克顿考虑了所有的方案，然后决定不应该让林肯冒这个险。他建议林肯改变自己的日程计划，同时不对外宣扬。平克顿认为林肯应该立刻动

assassin *n.* 刺客；暗杀者   attack *v.* 攻击；进攻
option *n.* 选择；选项   schedule *n.* 时间表

the change a secret. He said Lincoln should leave for Washington right away instead of waiting until the next morning. That way he would be in and out of Baltimore before Ferrandini's men ever knew about it.

Lincoln refused to do this. He had promised to attend two important events before leaving Pennsylvania. "Whatever the cost, these two promises I must *fulfill*," he told Pinkerton.

So Pinkerton tried again. Why not leave just 12 hours early? That way Lincoln could keep his promises, but still change his schedule enough to *evade* the killers. Lincoln agreed. Instead of leaving for Washington on the 23rd, he would leave late at night on the 22nd.

Secrecy was *vital*. Only a few people knew of the change in plans. To be extra safe, Pinkerton had the telegraph lines cut. That way if

---

身去华盛顿而不是等到第二天才出发，这样在费拉蒂尼他们察觉之前他就已经到达并且离开巴尔迪摩了。

但是林肯拒绝接受平克顿的建议，他已经承诺要在离开宾夕法尼亚之前出席两个重要的活动。所以他对平克顿说："无论做出多大的牺牲，我必须兑现我的这两个诺言。"

因此平克顿对方案又做出了调整，为什么不提前12个小时出发呢？那样的话林肯既可以履行自己的诺言，又可以改变时间表以此来躲过刺杀的人。林肯接受了这个建议，他们将在22日深夜出发而不是23日。

保密工作是十分重要的，只有几个人知道此次计划的改变。为了确保进一步的安全，平克顿又命令人把电报线掐断，这样的话即使有人发现了

---

fulfill *v.* 履行；实现
secrecy *n.* 保密

evade *v.* 逃避
vital *adj.* 至关重要的

anyone did find out about the change of plans, they couldn't warn the assassins.

To be sure no one noticed him, Lincoln traveled in a kind of *disguise*. He didn't wear his famous *stovepipe* hat. He wore a soft felt hat. He also tossed an overcoat *loosely* over his shoulders.

Just before midnight, Lincoln boarded a special train in Harrisburg, Pennsylvania. It would take him to Philadelphia. There a second train waited. This second train would whisk Lincoln straight to Washington, D.C.. It would pass through Baltimore, but he would not have to get out.

Still, there might be danger. Pinkerton feared the assassins would somehow learn of the change in plans. Then they could plant a *bomb* under one of the railroad bridges. They could kill Lincoln by

---

计划的改变，他们也不能再通知那些刺客了。

为了确保没有人会认出林肯，他在旅行时候还作了一些修饰——他没有戴他那著名的大礼帽，取而代之的是一顶呢帽；他又在肩头上松散地搭了一件大衣。

就在午夜之前，林肯登上了停在宾夕法尼亚哈里斯堡的一辆专列。这列火车将要载他去费城，在那里，另外一列火车正恭候着他。那列车会火速送他直接抵达哥伦比亚特区华盛顿，中途经过巴尔迪摩，但是林肯未必会离开火车。

尽管如此，还是会有危险存在。平克顿担心刺客说不准会从什么渠道就能得知计划的改变，然后在火车途径的桥上安装炸弹，用炸毁火车的手

---

disguise *n.* 伪装　　　　　　　　　　　　stovepipe *n.* 大礼帽

loosely *adv.* 宽松地　　　　　　　　　　bomb *n.* 炸弹

blowing up the whole train.

These doubts troubled Pinkerton. He wouldn't rest easy until the president was safely in Washington. So all night Pinkerton stood on the rear *platform* of Lincoln's special train. He had spies *stationed* all along the route. If there was any sign of trouble, they would signal Pinkerton. He would then immediately stop the train. *Fortunately*, there was no problem. The train arrived early the next morning in Washington.

There was one final scare, however. As Lincoln stepped off the train, a man shouted out to him. "Abe," he yelled, "you can't play that one on me." Pinkerton thought the stranger might be an assassin. He moved to attack him.

"Don't strike him!" *yelled* Lincoln. It turned out the stranger was a

---

段除掉林肯。

　　这些担忧困扰着平克顿。总统一时没有到达华盛顿，平克顿就一刻也不能高枕无忧。整个晚上，他都站在林肯专列后面车厢的连廊上。他要求手下在火车经过的沿途站好岗，一旦有任何风吹草动，马上发回通知，他好立刻让火车停下。万幸的是一路都平安无事，火车第二天一大早顺利抵达了华盛顿。

　　想不到最后还发生了一个小插曲，让人们虚惊一场。当林肯走出火车的时候，他听到有人喊："亚伯"——那是他的昵称。只见一个男子正朝着他大声叫嚷："你可骗不了我。"平克顿意识到这个人可能就是刺客，所以他赶了过去就要把那个叫嚷的人击倒。

　　此时林肯喊道："别打他。"原来这个陌生人是林肯的朋友，尽管林

---

platform　*n.* 月台；站台
fortunately　*adv.* 幸运地

station　*v.* 安置；驻扎
yell　*v.* 喊叫着说

friend of Lincoln's who had *recognized* him despite the disguise.

After people heard about the plot to kill Lincoln, the assassins went into hiding. They did not kill him. And they did not keep him from becoming president. Still, most Southerners *refused* to accept him as their leader. One after another, Southern states seceded from the Union. One month after Lincoln took office, the *Civil War* began.

The war lasted four long and *bloody* years. Then, just a few days after the war ended, John Wilkes Booth did what Ferrandini had failed to do. He shot President Lincoln in the back of the head on April 14, 1865. Allan Pinkerton was in Chicago when it happened. Sadly, he wasn't around to save Abraham Lincoln a second time.

肯化了妆，一下火车还是被这个朋友认出来了。

　　当人们得知有人要刺杀林肯的时候，刺客躲了起来，他们没有动手，他们也没能阻止林肯就任总统。但是南方人拒绝接受林肯作为他们的领导，他们一个州又一个州的从联盟中脱离了出去。就在林肯上任一个月后美国内战爆发了。

　　内战充满了血腥，一直持续了四年时间。然而就在战争结束以后没几天，约翰·威尔克斯·布斯完成了当年费兰蒂尼没有实现的任务——1865年4月14日那天，他用枪击中了林肯总统的后脑。枪击事件发生的时候，艾伦·平克顿正在芝加哥，不幸的是他没能第二次挽救亚伯拉罕·林肯。

---

recognize *v.* 认识；认得
civil war　内战

refuse *v.* 拒绝；不愿
bloody *adj.* 血腥的

The Miracle Mission

The B-17 bomber was like a *turtle*—slow and steady. It was meant to fly in a straight line to its *target*, drop its bombs, and fly in a straight line back home. The B-17 bomber had little *ability* to dodge enemy planes. And it surely couldn't *outrace* them. Yet this famed World

The B–17 bomber was not very fast, but it was hard to shoot down.

神奇使命

B17 型轰炸机飞行速度并不是很快，但是想要击落它们也不是那么容易。

B17轰炸机就像一只海龟，又慢又稳。它的任务就是一直飞到目的地，扔炸弹，然后再直接飞回来。B17轰炸机几乎没有能力来躲避敌人的敌机，当然它也不可能超越他们。然而，这些二战中闻名遐迩的飞机有着最为卓越的功能，那就是他们很难被击落。B17轰炸机经常满身弹孔或者有时候拖着残缺一大块的机翼、机尾返回基地。它们都配置了四个引擎，但是即使

turtle *n.* 龟；海龟
ability *n.* 能力；能耐

target *n.* 目标；靶子
outrace *v.* 胜过

War II plane had one *major* thing going for it. It was hard to shoot down. B-17s often returned to their bases shot full of holes or with a chunk of a wing or tail missing. The four-engine plane could *sputter* home even with one or two engines knocked out.

Lieutenant Edward Michael flew one of these tough B-17s. He named it *Bertie Lee* after his wife. On one bombing *mission*, the Bertie Lee came back with 144 holes in her. Then, on April 11, 1944, the plane *endured* its greatest test. So, too, did Lieutenant Michael.

That morning, he and his crew took off from England. The Bertie Lee was part of a 100-plane bombing run over Germany. Around 11 o'clock the planes arrived at their target. Shells from enemy guns on the ground began to burst all around them. They had no sure way to avoid this "flak." B-17 pilots just had to fly through it and hope they

是一个或两个引擎被打掉了，他们仍然能噼噼啪啪冒着火星返回来。

爱德华·麦克尔中尉就驾驶着这样一架轰炸机，他用自己妻子的名字贝蒂·李来命名自己的飞机。在一次轰炸任务中，贝蒂·李号曾经带着144个弹孔返回基地。然而在1944年4月11日那一天，她经受了一次最大的考验，一同经历考验的还有麦克尔中尉。

那天早晨，他和他的机组人员飞离了英格兰。这个由100架飞机组成的轰炸编队飞到了德国上空，贝蒂·李号就在其中。大约11点，编队到达了目的地，此时，地面上敌人的炮弹开始从四面八方向他们射来。B17没有稳妥的办法来躲避这些高射炮火，飞行员们只能在炮弹间穿行，期望能够避免中弹。危险接踵而至，德军的飞机也开始向轰炸机发动袭击，B17

major *adj.* 主要的
mission *n.* 使命；任务

sputter *v.* 发噼啪声
endure *v.* 忍耐；耐住

were not hit. That wasn't the only danger. German planes began to attack the bombers. Machine gunners on board the B-17s fired back.

The best defense the bombers had was to stick together. If they stayed in formation, they could protect each other. But that wasn't always possible. If a B-17 got hit, it might lose power and be unable to keep up. That's what happened to the *Bertie Lee*. Enemy fire riddled the plane with holes from its nose to its tail. The plane lost *altitude*. It fell out of *formation*. The *Bertie Lee* was now on its own. The *lumbering* bomber was like a duck in a shooting gallery.

Sensing an easy score, German pilots moved in to finish off the plane. One of their shells blew up the *Bertie Lee*'s *cockpit*. The explosion wounded copilot Franklin Westberg. It injured Edward Michael too. A piece of shrapnel cut deep into his right thigh. The

---

上的机枪手向德军开火予以还击。

　　对于B17轰炸机来说，最好的抵御方法就是聚集在一起。如果能保持编队的阵型不变，他们就可以互相保护。但是这个办法并非总是奏效的，如果一架B17中弹，他就要失去动力而掉队。这次，不幸降临到了贝蒂·李号身上，敌人的炮火把她从前端到尾部射出了无数的弹孔。贝蒂·李无法再继续保持原有高度，她不得不撤出编队，完全依靠自己了。现在，这架行动迟缓的轰炸机就像一只射击场上随时可能被射杀的鸭子。

　　看到贝蒂·李号已经成了煮熟的鸭子，德军开始打击她。先是一枚炮弹击中了飞机的座舱，而后炸伤了副驾驶员富兰克林·威斯特博格。同时，这枚炸弹也伤到了爱德华·麦克尔，一块榴霰弹的弹片深深地钻进了他的右大腿里。炮弹也炸毁了一侧的窗户并且毁坏了大部分的仪器设备。

---

altitude *n.* 高地；高度　　　　　　　　formation *n.* 编队

lumbering *adj.* 笨拙的；动作迟缓的　　　cockpit *n.* 驾驶员座舱

blast blew out a side window and wiped out most of the instruments. *Hydraulic* fluid *splattered* the windshield, making it hard to see. Black smoke filled the cockpit, obscuring vision even more. But this was just the beginning. Things were about to get much worse.

Michael got a frantic call from the men stationed back in the bomb bay. This was the section of the B-17 where the bombs were stored. The men reported that the bomb bay was on fire. Three shells had hit it, setting it ablaze. The bomb bay was still loaded with 100-pound bombs. These would burn *fiercely* if the fire reached them. Also, the plane's gas tanks were nearby. If the fire reached the tanks, the entire plane would explode.

Michael ordered his crew to drop all the bombs. But the *release lever* was jammed. The men couldn't get the bombs out.

Even though Michael was still over enemy land, he ordered

压力下的液体爆裂出来喷溅到挡风玻璃上，导致眼前一片模糊。整个驾驶舱里面都是黑烟，已经分辨不出东南西北了。但是，这仅仅是个开始，情况变得越来越糟糕。

与此同时，炸弹仓里面的士兵向他报告了一条让他几乎发疯的消息——那里面着火了。炸弹仓是B17存放炸弹的地方，现在它被敌人的三枚炮弹击中，开始冒火。如果火引燃了那里面100磅的炸弹，后果不堪设想。而且旁边就是飞机的油箱，一旦火烧到了油箱，结果就是机毁人亡。

麦克尔命令他的部下把所有的炮弹都丢下飞机。但是解锁手柄被卡住了，士兵无法把炮弹弄出来。

飞机现在还在敌人的地盘上，麦克尔命令部下跳伞逃离飞机，他觉得

---

hydraulic *adj.* 液压的   splatter *v.* 溅湿；溅脏

fiercely *adv.* 猛烈地   release lever 解锁手柄

everyone else in the plane to *bail out*. He thought it was their best chance of staying alive. Seven of his men *parachuted*. (They all survived, were *captured* by Germans, and became prisoners of war.) But two men refused to leave him. They were his copilot, Franklin Westberg, and *bombardier* John Lieber.

Lieber grabbed a machine gun and began firing at German planes. Michael saw Lieber and told him to jump. But Leiber's parachute was full of bullet holes. That made it useless. So Michael offered Leiber his own parachute.

"No, Mike," replied Leiber. "If we can't go out together, we'll go down together." Westberg also refused to jump. Each man acted out of his sense of duty toward the other two. So, with three men and only two parachutes, they all agreed to stay with the *Bertie Lee*.

这是活命的最好机会了。七名士兵跳伞离开了飞机（他们都活了下来，但是被德军俘获，成为战俘。），但是还有两个人拒绝离开麦克尔，他们就是副驾驶富兰克林·威斯特博格和投弹员约翰·利伯尔。

利伯尔夺过一架机枪开始向德军射击，麦克尔看到他后让他也跳伞离开。但是利伯尔的降落伞都是弹孔，已经不能使用了，麦克尔就把自己的降落伞给他。

利伯尔回答道："不，麦克。如果我们不能一起逃生，我们就死在一起。"威斯特博格也拒绝跳伞。每个人都对另外的两个人充满了责任感，因此，尽管三个人仅有两张降落伞，他们决定要与贝蒂·李号同生共死。

---

bail out 跳伞

capture *v.* 捕获；俘获

parachute *v.* 跳伞

bombardier *n.* 投弹手

Michael's instrument panel had been destroyed by German shells, so he was now flying "blind". He had no way of knowing his exact position. He just pointed his plane northwest toward England and hoped the *Bertie Lee* made it there.

Meanwhile, Lieber walked through the plane *putting out flames*. More flak rocked the B-17. Michael took the plane down very close to the ground to avoid it. That seemed to work. But soon enemy soldiers on the ground opened fire on the plane with their *rifles*.

Michael brought the plane up again. But when he reached an altitude of 2,500 feet, enemy fighters were waiting for him. He had to maneuver the plane to *evade* German fire from the ground and from the air. At times, he dropped the plane so low it clipped the tops of trees. Up and down Michael flew, using every trick he knew. Once

---

麦克尔的仪表盘已经被德军的炮弹炸毁了，所以他现在只能"盲飞"。由于无法得知自己的准确位置，他只得调转机头朝着西北的英格兰方向飞行，希望自己的贝蒂·李号能平安回到祖国。

此时，利伯尔穿过机舱来扑灭飞机上的大火。越来越多的高射炮震颤着这架B17，麦克尔让飞机尽可能低地贴着地面飞行以躲避敌军的炮火。然而很快敌军就用他们的步枪向贝蒂·李号射击。

麦克尔只好再一次把飞机提升起来。但是当他到达2500英尺高度的时候，敌军的歼击机正等候在那里，他只好策略地躲避着来自空中和地面的双重火力。麦克尔使出浑身解数来摆脱敌人，有时候飞机低到擦着树梢

---

put out 熄灭；扑灭　　　　　　　　　　　flame *n.* 火焰
rifle *n.* 步枪　　　　　　　　　　　　　evade *v.* 逃避

he even flew straight into a bank of clouds to lose a German fighter plane that was closing in on him.

At last, the *Bertie Lee* made it to the North Sea. A short time later, Michael saw the English coast. They were out of enemy *territory*! Once again, Michael instructed Lieber and Westberg to take the two good parachutes and jump to safety. But again, they refused to leave him. They were in this together and they would take their chances—with him—on a crash landing.

By this time, Lieutenant Michael was feeling very weak. The *gash* in his thigh had caused him to lose a lot of blood. Finally he lost *consciousness* and Westberg had to take over the controls. Just as the plane *approached* the landing field, Michael regained consciousness. He had enough strength left to try the landing himself.

掠过；有时候又直飞云端以甩掉敌机的追击。

　　终于，贝蒂·李成功的逃到了北海。不久以后，麦克尔看到了英国的海岸，他们终于逃出了敌人的控制范围。麦克尔再一次命令利伯尔和威斯特博格用那两个尚完好的降落伞逃生，但是他们又一次拒绝了中尉的要求。他们决定和麦克尔一起抓住这最后的机会——强行着陆。

　　此时，麦克尔中尉感觉到十分虚弱，大腿上深深的伤口已经流了很多血。最后他昏迷了过去，驾驶的任务只得由威斯特博格来完成。就在飞机要接近地面的时候，麦克尔重新恢复了意识，他用尽了剩下的力气又接过了操纵飞机的任务。

---

territory *n.* 领土；领域
consciousness *n.* 意识

gash *n.* 切口；切痕
approach *v.* 接近

It had to be a crash landing. The bomb bay doors were stuck open. The wing flaps didn't work. The wheels were useless without a hydraulic system. Yet despite the odds, Michael managed to make a perfect belly landing. The *Bertie Lee* and its three-man crew had made it. Soldiers at the base called it "The *Miracle* Mission." None of them could believe that a plane so badly shot up could still fly and land safely.

It took Lieutenant Edward Michael months to recover. Then, on January 10, 1945, he visited the *White House*. There he received the Medal of Honor—the nation's highest award. President Franklin D. Roosevelt shook his hand. It was quite an honor. But Michael had one regret. He wished John Lieber and Franklin Westberg had been given medals too. He knew in his heart that they *deserved* medals just as much as he did.

飞机必须强行着陆了，炸弹舱的舱门被撞开；飞机的两翼已经不好用了；没有了液压系统，飞机轮子也彻底报废。然而尽管成功的可能性很渺茫，麦克尔还是做出了完美的腹部着陆。贝蒂·李号和她的三名机组人员完成了着陆。基地的士兵几乎都不敢相信受到这样重创的飞机还能够飞回来并且安全着陆，他们都把这次返航叫作"神奇使命"。

爱德华·麦克尔的伤口几个月以后才得以康复。而后，在1945年1月10日那天，他拜访了美国的白宫。在那里他获得了国家最高的奖赏——荣誉勋章。富兰克林·D·罗斯福总统亲自和他握手，这是至高无上的荣誉。但是麦克尔有一点点遗憾，他希望约翰·利伯尔和富兰克林·威斯特博格也能得到同样的待遇。他知道在他的心里，他们两人和他本人一样，都配得上获得这样的勋章。

---

miracle *n.* 奇迹　　　　　　　　　　　　White House 白宫
deserve *v.* 应得；该得

8

Alone at Sea

Suppose you are lost at sea. You're *floating* on a *raft* in the middle of the ocean with no fresh water to drink. What should you do? Should you drink from the sea? If you do, will you go mad? Will you die a terrible, *agonizing* death?

Over the years many sailors have

Dr. Alain Bombard crossed the Atlantic Ocean in this small raft to prove that people could survive indefinitely while drinking salt water.

劈波斩浪

　　阿兰·鲍姆巴德医生就是乘坐这样的小筏子穿过了大西洋，以此证明了人在饮用海水的情况下也有可能生存下来。

　　假设你在大海中迷失了方向，你坐在一艘漂浮在大洋中的橡皮筏子里，而船上也没有了淡水，你会怎么做呢？你会不会喝海水呢？如果你喝了，你会不会变得疯狂了呢？你会不会在极度恐怖和痛苦中死去呢？

　　在过去数年中，许多在大海中迷失方向的水手都拒绝饮用就在他们周

---

float *v.* 漂浮 　　　　　　　　　　　　　　　　　raft *n.* 筏；木筏
agonizing *adj.* 苦恼的；折磨人的

been lost at sea. And most of them have refused to drink the salt water that was all around them. They believed they would die if they did. They thought drinking water from the ocean would drive them crazy with thirst and would *hasten* their deaths. Many knew of shipwrecked sailors who had, in *desperation*, *consumed* salt water. These men had been racked with terrible pains. They went out of their minds and finally died.

Because of such tales, most stranded sailors avoided drinking even small amounts of salt water. They just waited in misery while their bodies slowly became *dehydrated*. A human being can live 30 days without food. But a person can live only 10 days without water.

Alain Bombard, a 27-year-old French doctor, wanted to save the lives of shipwrecked sailors. He felt it was a mistake for them not to

---

围的海水，他们相信如果喝了就会死掉。他们也认为海水会让他们由于口渴变得疯狂进而加速死亡。很多人都听说过关于船只失事的报道，上面的船员在绝望中饮用了海水。这些船员都遭受了痛苦可怕的折磨，然后失去理智在痛苦中死去。

因为有了这些传说，大多数在困境中的船员哪怕连一小口海水都避免去喝，他们只能在痛苦中等待着身体慢慢脱水。人类在没有食物的条件下，可以生存30天。但是如果没有水，一个人只能活10天。

27岁的法国医生阿兰·鲍姆巴德决定要挽救那些失事海船上的生命。他觉得船员们不喝海水是错误的，事实上他认为船员们在身体脱水之

---

hasten *v.* 加速；加紧

consume *v.* 吃光；喝光

desperation *n.* 绝望的境地

dehydrated *adj.* 脱水的

drink seawater. In fact, he thought they should begin drinking it right away, before they became dehydrated. If they did that, he thought, their bodies could handle the extra salt. Then they could live much longer than 10 days.

To prove his point, Bombard decided to "*shipwreck*" himself. His plan was to drink a bit of seawater every day. Beyond that, he would get some water by *squeezing* the liquid out of fish he caught. Finally, he might pick up some rainwater here and there. Bombard was confident he could survive many days this way. But when he told people about his plan, they thought he was out of his mind.

On May 25, 1952, Bombard started his test. He cast himself *adrift* in the Mediterranean Sea in a rubber boat. A sailor named Jack Palmer went with him. The test was a *flop*. "The winds and

---

前可以用正确的方法饮用海水。而且如果海员们喝了海水的话，他们的身体可以处理掉多余的盐分，这样他们生存的时间就会远远多于10天。

为了证明自己的观点是正确的，鲍姆巴德决定让自己也"失事"一次。他的计划是每天饮用一点海水；此外他还喝一些从他捕获的鱼身上榨出的水分；最后，他还可以到处获取一些降落的雨水。鲍姆巴德相信用这种方法他可以生存许多天。但是当他把这个计划告诉别人的时候，人们都认为他一定是发疯了。

鲍姆巴德于1952年5月25日开始了他的测试。他乘坐一艘橡皮船在地中海上漂浮，同行的还有一名叫杰克·帕默的水手。试验最后以失败而告终。鲍姆巴德说："风和水流让我们在海上兜了几天的圈子。"更糟糕的

---

shipwreck *v.* 使失事　　　　　　　　　　squeeze *v.* 挤压

adrift *adv.* 漂浮着　　　　　　　　　　　flop *n.* 失败

currents drove us in circles for days," Bombard said. Worse still, the Mediterranean Sea didn't contain many fish. Bombard and Palmer had trouble catching enough to stay alive. Still, they survived more than two weeks. Drinking the salt water didn't make them crazy. But the *voyage* wasn't much fun.

Still, Bombard wasn't ready to give up. In fact, he wanted to try floating his raft across the *entire* Atlantic Ocean. Jack Palmer, on the other hand, had seen enough. He thought it would be *suicide* to head out across the ocean without fresh water.

So on October 19, 1952, Bombard set out across the Atlantic alone. He sailed in a 15-foot rubber boat. It had a wooden floor and a small mast. If Bombard made it all the way to the West Indies, he would have proved his *theory*. If he died, at least he felt his death

是地中海里没有太多的鱼，鲍姆巴德和帕默很难捕捉到足够的鱼来充饥，然而他们还是生存了两周多的时间。最后，喝海水没有让他们发疯，但是这次航海却没有给他们留下太多愉快的记忆。

　　然而鲍姆巴德并没有准备放弃他的测试计划，并想要驾驶自己的橡皮筏子横渡整个大西洋。另一方面，杰克·帕默感觉漂流地中海已经足够了，他认为没有淡水的情况下横渡大西洋无异于自杀。

　　因此1952年10月19日那一天，在没有人陪伴的情况下鲍姆巴德开始了他独自穿越大西洋的航程。他驾驶着一艘15英尺长的橡皮船，船上铺着木质底板还装有一根小桅杆。如果小船能够顺利抵达西印度群岛，这将证明他的理论是正确的；如果他不幸遇难，他觉得至少他的死是很有价值的。

voyage *n.* 航行；航程
suicide *n.* 自杀

entire *adj.* 全部的；整个的
theory *n.* 原理；理论

would be for a noble cause.

Bombard did carry some food and water with him. He could use them to save his life. But if he did, his voyage would be a failure. To make sure no one could later *claim* he cheated, Bombard had officials lock the supplies with a special *seal*. If the seal was broken, everyone would know his theory had failed.

Other than these emergency supplies, Bombard took no food and no water. His food and drink would have to come from the sea. On this journey, he had no problem finding food. "There were plenty of fish," Bombard said. "Little flying fish struck against my sail and fell in the raft." He also fished with a *makeshift harpoon*. Of course, he had no stove. So he ate the fish raw. The pink flesh didn't look very good, but he found that the taste wasn't bad.

鲍姆巴德的确携带了一些淡水和食物，他可以依赖这些东西在危难的情况下救命。但是如果他真的动了这些食物，他的航行就会变得没有意义。为了保证将来不会有人说他作弊，鲍姆巴德用一张特制的封条正式把这些水和食物封了起来。如果封条坏了，人们就会知道他的理论是站不住脚的。

除了这些紧急情况下才能动用的补充品之外，鲍姆巴德没有带任何其他的食物和水，他的饮食都必须取自于大海。在航行中，食物并没有给他带来太大的麻烦。"海上有足够的鱼供我享用。"他说，"小飞鱼有时候会撞到帆上然后跌入到我的舱中。"他也会使用临时的鱼叉来捕鱼。当然，他没有火炉，所以他只能吃生鱼。粉红色的鱼肉看起来让人难以下咽，但是他发现吃起来味道还不错。

---

claim *v.* 要求；声称　　　　　　　　　　　seal *n.* 封条
makeshift *adj.* 临时的　　　　　　　　　　harpoon *n.* 鱼叉

Bombard knew he couldn't live just on fish. If he did, he would get *scurvy*, a disease that comes from not getting the right vitamins. So Bombard *dragged* a piece of cloth behind the boat to catch plankton. Eating these tiny sea *creatures* helped to balance his diet.

For liquid, Bombard drank 1½ pints of seawater each day. He also drank the juice he squeezed from fish. "For 23 days I had no rainwater, but fish juices served the purpose. I had no trouble with real thirst."

Bombard did, however, have trouble with *loneliness*. At times he was frightened by the "terror of the open sea." He longed for the sound of human voices. The only noises he heard during his journey were "the rushing of the wind, the watery hiss of the breaking waves, [and] the nervous flutter of the sail."

鲍姆巴德知道他不能总靠吃鱼活着，否则他就会因为体内缺少一定的维生素患上坏血病。于是他把一块帆布拖在船尾来捕获一些海洋中的藻类等浮游生物。吃这些生物可以平衡一下他体内的营养。

至于口渴，鲍姆巴德每天都饮用1.5品脱的海水，他也喝从鱼身上挤出来的汁液。"23天一直都没有下雨，但是鱼身上的汁液可以代替雨水，口渴真的没有对我形成太大的麻烦。"

对于鲍姆巴德来说真正的麻烦来自于孤独。有时候他被"远洋恐惧症"所困扰，他渴望能听到人类的声音。航行期间唯一陪伴他的只有"风的呼啸声、海浪破碎时候的嘶嘶声以及船帆在风中不安的鼓动声。"

---

scurvy *n.* 坏血病

creature *n.* 动物；生物

drag *v.* 拖动

loneliness *n.* 寂寞；孤独

Early in his voyage, a storm almost destroyed his boat. Bombard had been sailing less than a week when the storm struck. Huge waves battered the boat. "One minute I perched atop [the waves] like a *surfboard*," he recalled, "the next, I was in a *hollow* so deep I could barely feel the wind." Strong winds ripped his sail. They also ruined his spare sail. Luckily, Bombard managed to sew the first sail back together again.

The next weeks passed quite *uneventfully*. Then, after about a month and a half, the wind suddenly died. Bombard's boat stopped moving. After several days of deadly calm, he began to fear he would never reach the West Indies. And if he died now, nobody would know that he had survived so long.

Then, at last, a British ship appeared on the *horizon*. The ship's captain couldn't believe Bombard was still alive. By this time

出发不到一周，他遇到了一场暴风雨，风暴和巨浪猛烈地摧残着这艘小船。事后鲍姆巴德回忆道："有时候我感觉到我就像一块冲浪板被推到了浪尖，片刻以后又落入了深深的波谷之中以至于我都感觉不到周围的风吹。"强风撕裂了他的船帆，也毁坏了备用帆。幸运的是鲍姆巴德把两面帆重新缝合到了一起。

接下来的几周都平安无事。但是就在他出发大约一个半月以后，海面上的风突然都消失得无影无踪，鲍姆巴德的船停止了前进。就这样在死一般的寂静中度过了几天，他开始担心永远也难以到达西印度群岛了。一旦他死掉，没有人会知道他曾经在海上独自一人生存了这么久。

终于，一艘英国海船在地平线上出现了。看到鲍姆巴德以后，海船

surfboard *n.* 冲浪板　　　　　　　　　　hollow *n.* 洞；山谷
uneventfully *adv.* 太平无事地　　　　　　horizon *n.* 地平线

the French doctor had been at sea for 53 days. Bombard was heartbroken to learn that he was still 600 miles from the West Indies. Still, he had *proven* his theory. According to the old belief, he should have died six weeks earlier.

Bombard could have ended his journey right then and there. But he wanted to continue on to the West Indies. So after a *meager* meal on board the ship, he climbed back into his boat. His spirits had been *restored*. Happily, the wind began to blow again.

On December 23, 1952, Dr. Alain Bombard reached the West Indies. He had been at sea for 65 days. He had sailed more than 2,750 miles and had lost 56 pounds. But he was alive. He had proven his theory! And, just in case someone *doubted* him, the seal on his emergency supplies was unbroken.

船长简直无法相信他还活着。此时这位法国医生已经在海上漂流了53天。当他听说这里距离西印度群岛还有600英里的时候，他感到非常悲伤。但是他已经证明了他的理论，如果根据旧的观念，他在6周以前就应该死掉了。

鲍姆巴德本可以就此结束他的航程了，但是他不想放弃，他想亲自完成这次航海任务。这样，在海船上简单地吃了一顿饭后他又返回了自己的小船上。现在他的精神已经恢复，同样幸运的是海面上的风也开始吹了起来。

阿兰·鲍姆巴德医生于1952年12月23日顺利抵达西印度群岛。他一共用了65天时间在海上漂流了2750英里，同时他也掉了56磅重的分量。但是他仍然活着，他也证明了自己的理论。如果有人质疑他的话，就让他们看一看那些紧急备用食品吧，那上面的封条依然完好无损。

---

prove *v.* 证明
restore *v.* 修复；恢复健康

meager *adj.* 质量差的；粗劣的
doubt *v.* 怀疑

9

Escape from Iran

It came as a total shock. No one is ever supposed to *attack* the *embassy* of another country. But that is what happened late in the morning of November 4, 1979. A *mob* of people filled the streets in Tehran, the capital city of Iran. They stormed the United States Embassy. They climbed

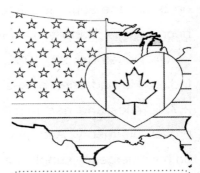

Americans put up signs to thank Canadians for their help in getting six trapped Americans out of Iran.

"朗"口脱险

美国人挂起招牌来感谢加拿大人，因为他们曾经帮助六名身陷险境的美国人逃离了伊朗。

突然而来的袭击震惊了几乎所有的人——没有人会想到一个国家的大使馆会遭到所在国居民的袭击。1979年11月4日接近中午的时候，在伊朗首都德黑兰，这个事件变成了事实。一群暴徒涌上了街道，他们像暴风雨般冲向美国驻伊朗大使馆，挥舞着手里的枪支，翻过大使馆的墙，疯狂地喊着，"让美国人去死吧!"

attack *v.* 攻击　　　　　　　　　　　　　embassy *n.* 大使馆
mob *n.* 一群暴徒

over the walls and waved guns in the air. They shouted, "Death to America!"

In just a few minutes, the Iranians took control of the embassy. They *captured* 52 Americans there. These men and women would be held prisoners for the next 444 days. But six Americans escaped the mob. They slipped out a back door. They ran into the street. They didn't know which way to turn. All they knew was that they were not safe. If anyone saw them, they would be taken *hostage*. They might even be killed.

Desperate, the six men and women went to the Canadian Embassy. They asked the Canadians to hide them. It was not a *simple favor*. If the Canadians agreed, they would be risking their own lives. The Iranians might find out. They might attack the Canadians.

　　数分钟以后，伊朗人控制了大使馆。他们在那俘获了52名美国人。这些美国人随即变成了俘虏，一直到444天以后才重新获得自由。但是，六名美国人还是从这些暴徒的手里逃掉了，他们偷偷地从后门溜了出来然后跑到街上。他们并不知道走哪条路，他们所知道的就是自己仍然身处危险之中。如果被伊朗人发现，他们就会被押做人质，甚至有可能被杀掉。

　　绝望之中，这六个美国人跑进了加拿大大使馆，请求加拿大人收留他们。但是这个忙不是随随便便就能够帮的，如果加拿大人同意庇护美国人，他们就得冒生命的危险，因为一旦被伊朗人发现，他们同样会袭击加拿大人。

---

capture　*v.* 捕获；俘获　　　　　　　　　　hostage　*n.* 人质
simple　*adj.* 简单的；基本的　　　　　　　　favor　*n.* 帮助；恩惠

Canada's *Ambassador*, Ken Taylor, knew that. He gathered his staff and told them about the dangers. Then he asked them what he should do. The Canadians didn't flinch. They wanted to help. Some even offered to hide Americans in their own homes. Taylor and his wife did this. They hid Joseph and Kathy Stafford.

Taylor's staff hoped to *smuggle* the six Americans out of Iran to safety. But how? The airports and train stations were closely watched. Any American trying to leave would be quickly *arrested*. So Taylor watched and waited. He sent some of his staff out of the country on unnecessary trips. He did this to find out how hard it would be to *sneak* someone out of Iran. He also wanted airport officials in Iran to get used to Canadians going in and out of the country.

加拿大大使肯·泰勒深知当前的处境。他把使馆的工作人员都召集起来通知了他们当前的危险处境。然后他告诉了手下他的想法。加拿大人没有退缩，他们决定帮助美国人。有些加拿大人甚至要让美国人住在自己的家里。泰勒和他的妻子也收留了两个美国人——约瑟夫和凯西·斯塔福德。

泰勒的手下希望能把这些美国人偷偷地带出伊朗，但是用什么方法呢？机场和火车站都已经被紧密地监视起来，只要有美国人离开马上就会被逮捕。泰勒在观望中等待着，他让部分工作人员通过一些没有必要的途径离开伊朗，想以此来弄清楚暗中把美国人送出伊朗的可能性有多大。他也想让伊朗的机场官员习惯于看到加拿大人在这个国家进进出出。

---

ambassador *n.* 大使；代表
arrest *v.* 逮捕

smuggle *v.* 走私；偷运
sneak *v.* 私运；偷带

Meanwhile, back in the United States, Antonio Mendez learned about the six men and women. Mendez worked for the CIA, America's spy agency. Mendez went to work on his own *scheme* for helping the six Americans. He talked to officials in Canada. He got them to issue six *fake* Canadian passports. The Americans would need these if they had any hope of slipping out of Iran.

Then Mendez dreamed up a *bold* plan. It was like something out of a movie. Mendez pretended to be an Irish filmmaker. He had to make Iranians believe he really was making a film. So he opened an office for his *phony* company. He hired people to work for it. Mendez

---

与此同时，美国国内的安东尼奥·曼德斯也得知现在这六个美国人的处境。曼德斯为美国的间谍机构——中央情报局效力，他自己制订了援救六名美国人的计划。他先联系了加拿大的官员，让他们伪造出六份假的加拿大护照，当美国人溜出伊朗的时候也许这些假护照会派上用场。

然后曼德斯构思出了一个大胆的计谋。一切就像电影中上演的一样，曼德斯装作是一位爱尔兰的电影制片人。为了取得伊朗人的信任，他为他的假冒公司在伊朗设立了一间办公室并且招募了若干工作人员。他把这部子虚乌有的电影定位为科幻恐怖片，并且给它起名"阿尔戈号"。曼德斯还创作出一幕情节，它要求在德黑兰拍摄一些场景。

---

scheme *n.* 计划
bold *adj.* 大胆的；勇敢的

fake *adj.* 伪造的
phony *adj.* 假的；欺骗的

decided his bogus film would be a science fiction thriller. He called it *Argo*. He *created* a *script* that called for some scenes to be shot in Tehran.

During this time, things remained tense for the six Americans and their Canadian hosts. All of them were afraid their secret would be *discovered*. On January 19, 1980, their fears came true. On that day Taylor's wife, Patricia, got a phone call.

"May I speak to Mr. or Mrs. Stafford?" the caller asked.

The question shook Patricia. No one knew that Joseph and Kathy Stafford were hiding in her house.

"I'm sorry," she said, trying to sound calm. "There is no one by that name living here."

But the caller *repeated* his question. He said he knew that the

---

在此期间，六个美国人和收留他们主人的周围情况依然十分紧张，他们都担心秘密会暴露出去。1980年1月19日那天，担心的事情终于成为现实。泰勒的妻子帕特丽夏当天接到了一个电话。

打电话的人问她："是斯塔福德先生或者斯塔福德夫人吗？"
这个问话使得帕特丽夏为之一颤。没有人知道约瑟夫和凯西·斯塔福德藏在她家。

所以她竭力用平稳的口气回答说："很抱歉，这里没有叫这个名字的人。"

但是打电话的人仍然重复着同样的问题。他说他知道斯坦福德就在这

---

create *v.* 创造；建立　　　　　　　　　script *n.* 脚本
discover *v.* 发现；找到　　　　　　　　repeat *v.* 重复

Staffords were there. At last, Patricia *hung up*.

The six Americans were now in great danger. They would have to get out of Iran, and they would have to move fast. The Canadians would have to clear out too. The Iranians might attack them for helping the Americans. Over the next few days, Taylor *sent* many of his staff members on trips out of Iran. None of them came back. Soon he had only four people left on his staff at the embassy.

At that point, Antonio Mendez *showed up*. He had gotten into Iran without any trouble. After all, his phony passport showed that he was Irish, not American. Mendez told Iranian *officials* he had come to work on his film. But he told Taylor the truth. He had come to help get the six Americans out of the country.

Taylor got Mendez and the Americans together. Mendez gave

里。最后，帕特丽夏把电话挂断了。

现在六名美国人的处境极其危险，他们必须离开伊朗，而且越快越好。加拿大人也不能在这里逗留了，伊朗人也许会因为他们帮助了美国人而向他们发动攻击。在随后的几天里，泰勒让他的很多随从离开了伊朗，不许再回来。很快，在大使馆里他的身边只剩下三名工作人员了。

就在这个紧张的关头，安东尼奥·曼德斯出现了。他没费什么力气就进入了伊朗，毕竟他的假护照上面表明他是一名爱尔兰人而不是美国人。曼德斯告诉伊朗官员自己是来拍摄电影的。但是他告诉了泰勒事情的真相——他是来帮助六名美国人离开伊朗的。

泰勒把曼德斯和六名美国人聚到了一起。曼德斯给这些美国人发了加

---

hang up 挂断
show up 露面；露出

send *v.* 送；寄出
official *n.* 官员

them Canadian passports. He told them they were going to pose as members of his fake film company. Kathleen Stafford, for instance, would be the *Argo set designer*. Cora Lijek would be a *screenwriter*.

Mendez helped the Americans dress for their parts. He had Mark Lijek *dye* his beard black. He gave Kathleen Stafford a thick pair of glasses to wear. Bob Anders usually dressed in dark suits. But Mendez had him put on tight pants and a blue silk shirt that was open at the top. Mendez puffed up Anders's hair into a big wave. He put a *flashy* gold chain around his neck.

On January 28 the Americans went to the airport. Dressed as part of the *Argo* crew, they headed for a flight out of the country. As Mendez held his breath, they flashed their Canadian passports. The Iranians never gave them a second look. They all got on a plane for

---

拿大的护照并且让他们装作是自己冒牌电影公司中的工作人员。比如，凯思琳·斯塔福德是电影"阿尔戈号"的布景师，科拉·里杰克则是电影的编剧。

曼德斯又帮助他们根据各自的角色打扮了一番。他让马克·里杰克把自己的胡子染成黑色；又给了凯思琳·斯塔福德一副厚厚的眼镜让她戴上。鲍勃·安德斯通常穿着深色的套装，但是曼德斯让他穿上一条紧身裤和一件套头的蓝色丝绸衬衫，又把他的头发吹成大波浪，还让他在脖子上戴了一条耀眼的金项链。

美国人在1月28日赶往飞机场，他们是以"阿尔戈号"剧组成员的身份准备登机出国的。当他们出示自己的加拿大护照的时候，伊朗人甚至都

---

set designer 布景师
dye *v.* 染；把……染上颜色

screenwriter *n.* 编剧家
flashy *adj.* 闪光的

Germany and *freedom*. The same day, Taylor and his last three staff members quietly flew to Europe also.

It took the Iranians a while to figure out what had happened. When they did, they were *furious*. Their outrage was aimed at the Canadians. They branded Taylor and his staff outlaws. They even issued threats against Canada. A spokesman for Iran declared, "Sooner or later, somewhere in the world, Canada will pay for this *crime*."

To Americans, though, the Canadians were heroes. Taylor and his staff had risked their lives to help six frightened souls get out of Iran. Americans flooded the Canadian government with thank-you cards. They flew Canadian *flags* next to American ones. And all across the United States, people put up big signs that said, "Thank You, Canada."

没有看他们第二眼。他们都登上了飞往德国也是飞往自由的航班。同一天，泰勒和剩下的三名使馆工作人员也悄无声息地飞往了欧洲。

伊朗人过了一段时间才发现情况不妙。当得知真相的时候，他们极为愤怒。他们把愤怒的矛头直指加拿大人。伊朗人辱骂泰勒和他的工作人员是逃犯。他们甚至向加拿大发出威胁，一名伊朗发言人宣称："迟早有一天，加拿大人要为他们所犯下的罪行付出代价。"

然而对于美国人来说，加拿大人是英雄。泰勒和他的手下冒着生命危险帮助六个恐惧中的美国人逃离了伊朗。写有感谢字样的卡片像洪水一般涌向了加拿大政府。他们就在星条旗旁悬挂着加拿大的国旗。整个国家到处都有人们悬挂的标语，上面写道;"感谢你，加拿大。"

---

freedom *n.* 自由；自主　　　　　　furious *adj.* 暴怒的；狂怒的
crime *n.* 罪行；犯罪　　　　　　　flag *n.* 旗帜

71

It was years before the world *found out* that the CIA had also *taken part in* the scheme. Antonio Mendez had *sworn* an oath of secrecy. So no one knew what *role* he had played. No one stopped to shake his hand in the street. He got no signs or thank-you notes. And that was just fine with him. From his point of view, his daring actions had just been part of the job.

　　几年以前全世界才知道是中央情报局参与了这次救援行动。但是安东尼奥·曼德斯曾经发过誓保守这个秘密，所以没有人知道他在这次行动中扮演了什么角色；没有人在大街上停下来和他握一握手，也没有人给他写下充满感激的只言片语。但是对于他来说这是很不错的，从他的观点来看，这次勇敢的行动只不过是他工作的一部分。

---

find out　找出；查明　　　　　　　　　　take part in　参加；参与
swear　*v.* 发誓　　　　　　　　　　　　　role　*n.* 角色；任务

10

Fearless Reporter

One night in January 1995, Veronica Guerin heard a knock on the front door of her home in Dublin, Ireland. She opened the door. "The first thing my eyes were *drawn* to was a *handgun*," she said. Then she saw the man standing there, pointing the gun *directly* at her. "I looked up to

Veronica Guerin is pictured here with her son, Cathal, and her husband, Graham Turley.

勇者无惧

维罗妮卡·格林与他的儿子凯瑟尔以及丈夫格雷厄姆·图雷的合影。

1995年1月的一天晚上，家在爱尔兰首都都柏林的维罗妮卡·格林听到有人在敲她家的前门，于是她打开了门。"我第一眼看见的是一把手枪，"她事后说道。而后她看到一名男子站在那里正用枪指着她。"我抬

draw *v.* 吸引　　　　　　　　　handgun *n.* 手枪
directly *adv.* 直接地

his eyes to *appeal* to him—don't, don't shoot me." Then, expecting to die, she *collapsed* on the floor. The man pointed the gun at her head. But after a moment he *lowered* it and shot her in the thigh.

The bullet was meant to send a message. She had better stop writing about crime kingpins. Guerin was a reporter for the *Sunday Independent*, Ireland's most widely read newspaper. The day she was shot, one of her articles appeared. It was about a top criminal she called Monk. That wasn't his real name. Libel laws in Ireland are strict, so Guerin used *nicknames*. Still, it wasn't hard for people to figure out who Monk was.

The bullet in the thigh was not the first time some gangster tried to intimidate Guerin. In September 1994, she had written an article about the "General." This gangster had recently been shot dead

---

头看着他的眼睛，向他恳求——不要，不要杀我。"然后她倒在了地上，以为自己已经死了。男子用枪指着她的头部，但是过了一会他把枪朝下挪，在格林的大腿上开了一枪。

子弹是给格林一个警告，让她最好不要再撰写关于一些重要人物的犯罪报道。格林是爱尔兰发行量最大的报纸《星期天独立报》的记者。她遭受枪击那天，正是她的一篇报道发表的日子。在这片文章中她报道一个名叫"僧侣"而且地位很高的罪犯。僧侣不是那名罪犯的本名，那是格林给他起的绰号。在爱尔兰诽谤的惩处是很严厉的。但是明白人都能看出来这个僧侣指的是谁。

大腿中枪已经不是格林第一次受到歹徒的恐吓了。1994年9月，她写文章报道了一个名叫"将军"的犯罪分子的劣行，这个家伙那个时候刚刚

---

appeal *v.* 恳求

lower *v.* 降低

collapse *v.* 倒下

nickname *n.* 绰号

in his car. Her story must have upset some members of his gang. About a month later, Guerin was playing with her young son at home. Suddenly, someone fired a bullet through her front window. Luckily, no one was hurt.

The bullet through the window had not stopped Guerin. And neither did the slug in her thigh. Veronica Guerin was not easily frightened. While still recovering from her leg wound, she left the hospital on *crutches*. Then she told her husband to drive her to see every big crime figure she knew. She wanted to show them she couldn't be *intimidated*. "This is it," she explained to her husband. "I'm going to let [them] see they didn't get to me."

One *threat*, however, did almost get to her. Nine months after she was shot in the thigh she went to see John Gilligan, a *mobster* who

---

在车中被人射杀。但是文章使得"将军"的手下惶惶不安。一个月以后的一天，正当格林和她年幼的儿子在家中玩耍的时候，一颗子弹击碎了前面窗户的玻璃。幸运的是没有人受到伤害。

穿过玻璃的子弹没有吓倒格林，嵌在大腿里面的弹片也没有让她退缩。维罗妮卡·格林不是轻易就胆怯的人。当她的腿伤还在恢复之中，她就拄着拐杖离开了医院。然后她让丈夫开车送自己去看她所知道的每一个犯罪的重要人物，以此来表明她不会被威胁吓倒。她对丈夫说："就这样吧。我要让他们看到他们永远都不能把我怎么样。"

然而有一个威胁的确影响了她。那是距她大腿受伤九个月以后，她前去采访刚刚出狱的犯罪集团成员约翰·吉里根。格林事先没有通知他就在

---

crutch *n.* 拐杖；支撑物　　　　　intimidate *v.* 威胁；恐吓
threat *n.* 威胁　　　　　　　　　mobster *n.* 匪徒；犯罪集团成员

had just gotten out of prison. She showed up at his *lavish* country *estate* without any notice. She asked Gilligan to explain how he could afford such a house. He had no job or any other legal *source* of wealth. Guerin's questions *enraged* Gilligan. He got so mad he ripped her shirt looking for a hidden microphone. He punched her in the face and chest. Then he screamed out a threat to kill her and her family.

Gilligan didn't stop there. The next day Guerin got a phone call from him. He whispered, "If you write one word about me, I will find your boy and kidnap him. I am going to shoot you, do you understand what I'm saying to you?" The direct threat to her 7-year-old son unnerved her. Still, she didn't quit investigating Gilligan.

In 1996 Guerin admitted that when she first started writing about

---

他的奢华庄园中出现了。她要吉里根解释如何支付得起这样一幢豪华的房产，而他既没有工作也没有合法的收入。格林的问题激怒了吉里根。他像疯了一样撕扯着格林的衣服，想要找到隐藏的麦克风。他猛烈地击打着她的脸和胸部，然后又叫嚷着要杀掉格林和她的全家。

吉里根并没有罢手。第二天，格林接到他打来的电话。他在电话里低低地对格林说："如果你敢写出一个和我有关的字，我就找到你的儿子绑架了他。我就要杀了你，你明白我说的意思吗？"对她七岁的儿子赤裸裸的威胁让格林惴惴不安。但是，她还是没有放弃对吉里根的调查。

1996年格林承认当她开始写文章报道毒品种植主和上层犯罪分子的

---

lavish *adj.* 充裕的；异常丰富的

source *n.* 来源

estate *n.* 庄园；种植园

enrage *v.* 使发怒；触怒

drug lords and other top criminals, she hadn't known how *scary* her job would turn out to be. If she had known, she said, "I would never have gotten into it. But having got into it, I cannot walk away from it. It's a job that must be done. And I'm a *journalist*."

Guerin believed her life was protected because she was a journalist. She didn't think any criminal would ever kill her. Yes, they might beat her and threaten her with death.

But no journalist had ever been killed in Ireland. There seemed to be some unwritten rule against it. So when Liam Collins, one of Guerin's editors, *cautioned* her not to take wild risks, she just brushed him off. "Ah, come on," she said.

Meanwhile, Guerin won lots of *praise* from fellow journalists. "Veronica Guerin got close to criminals in a way that had never been

时候，她并不知道这份工作将来会有多大的危险。如果当初她知道的话，她说："我就不会参与进来。但是既然已经进来，我就不打算离开了。因为这是一项必须完成的工作，而且因为我是一名记者。"

格林相信她的生命是受到保护的，因为她是记者。她认为没有犯罪分子会杀了她，也许他们会殴打她或者用死亡来威胁她。

但是在爱尔兰没有记者被杀害的先例，看起来这已经是不成文的规定。所以当她的一个编辑莱阿姆·科林斯警告她不要再冒险的时候，格林并没有在意他的话，只是说了一句："啊，没有关系的。"

同时，格林也获得了同行们的交口称赞。爱尔兰时报的麦克尔·福利赞扬道："维罗妮卡·格林用以前所未有的方式近距离地采访了这些罪

scary *adj.* 引起恐惧的；骇人的　　　　journalist *n.* 记者
caution *v.* 警告　　　　　　　　　　　praise *n.* 赞扬；表扬

done before," said Michael Foley of *The Irish Times*. That was why she got so many *scoops* — why so many of her stories made it to the front page.

After she was shot in the thigh, her newspaper put an expensive security system in her home. The police *guarded* her 24 hours a day. But that made it harder for Guerin to do her job. She couldn't get her informants to talk with the police around. Some of these people were small-time hoods. They didn't want to get near the police. But Guerin needed to talk to them in order to get information about the crime bosses. So she soon gave up her police *escort*. Later, she explained to her friends that no one could guarantee her safety. Even if she wore a *bulletproof* vest, she said, "I'd still have to take it off at night."

犯。"这也正是为什么她能够获得如此多的独家新闻，而她的报道又能经常在报纸的头版刊登。

在她的大腿受伤以后，报社在她家里安装了一套价格不菲的安全系统，还有一名警察24小时在身旁保护着她。但是这让她难以开展工作，和警察聊天是得不到她想要的信息的。格林需要从一些市井混混口中得到关于老板犯罪的资料，然而这些人不想看到身旁有警察。所以，格林很快就放弃了警察对她的安全保卫。她后来向朋友解释说没有人能够确保她的安全，即使她穿了一件防弹背心。她说："我晚上睡觉时总要把防弹衣脱了吧。"

---

scoop *n.* 独家新闻
escort *n.* 陪同；护送者

guard *v.* 保卫；看守
bulletproof *adj.* 防弹的

On June 26, 1996, Guerin had to go to court. She had recently gotten a ticket for speeding. She was worried that the judge might *suspend* her *license*. For Guerin, losing her license for three months or six months would have made her job difficult. Her car acted as a kind of mobile office. The judge, however, let Guerin off with a fine and a warning.

So Guerin was happy when she left the court. She headed back to the newspaper building. On the way, she stopped at a red light. As she waited she picked up her cell phone to call a friend. She didn't notice two men on a motorcycle pull up next to her. Suddenly, the man on the back of the bike jumped off. He pulled out a gun and fired five shots at her. The bullets *smashed* into her neck and chest. Veronica Guerin died *instantly*.

1996年6月26日，格林不得不走进法庭。由于超速驾驶她收到了法庭的传票，她担心法官会吊扣她的驾驶执照。对于格林来说，失去驾驶执照三个月或者六个月将会给她的工作带来不便，她的汽车扮演着移动办公室的作用。但是法官只是警告了她并且罚了些钱就让她走了。

离开法庭的时候，格林很高兴，她驾车返回报社大楼。路上她停在了一处红灯前面，她一边等待红灯，一边拿出手机给一个朋友打电话。就在这个时候，她没有注意到一辆载着两名男子的摩托车停在了她身边。突然，摩托车后座位上的男子跳了下来，拔出一把枪向着格林连开了五枪。子弹穿进了她的脖子和胸膛，维罗妮卡·格林当场就死掉了。

---

suspend *v.* 使暂停
smash *v.* 狠打；猛击

license *n.* 执照；许可证
instantly *adv.* 立即；马上

The murder shocked people around the world. John Bruton, the prime minister of Ireland, called the shooting "*sinister* in the extreme." The police launched a huge manhunt to find her killers. They put 60 detectives on the case. Guerin had made many enemies. So at first the police had a list of 150 *suspects*. It took them a while to find the right person.

In time, however, they *arrested* drug lord Paul Ward. In November 1998, he was tried and found guilty of *murder*. Ward was sentenced to life in prison.

刺杀行为震惊了整个世界。爱尔兰总理约翰·布鲁顿称这次枪击是"极端的罪恶。"警察局派出大量的人力追捕凶手，他们派出了60名侦探来侦破这个案件。由于格林树敌过多，因此开始的时候警察列了一份有150名嫌疑犯的大名单，他们又花费了一段时间才找到真正的凶手。

终于，警察逮捕了毒品种植主保罗·沃德。1998年11月，他在法庭受审并且被宣判谋杀罪成立，判终身监禁。

---

sinister *adj.* 阴险的；恶意的

arrest *v.* 逮捕

suspect *n.* 嫌疑犯

murder *n.* 谋杀

Nurses on the Front Line

They got sick just like the men. They were bombed and shot at just like the men. And they were taken *prisoners* of war just like the men. During World War II, American army nurses were right up on the *front lines*. About the only difference between a male *soldier* and a female

During World War II, nurses were on the front lines just like the soldiers. Here, Red Cross nurses march in formation.

战地护士

　　二战期间，护士和士兵一样都在前线。图片上，红十字会的护士们在列队前进。

　　她们就像男人一样接受病魔考验；她们就像男人一样接受炮火和子弹的洗礼；她们就像男人一样被虏为战俘。在二次大战期间，美国军队的护士同样在前线。男性士兵和女护士们之间唯一的不同就是护士们不扛枪。

---

prisoner *n.* 囚犯；犯人
soldier *n.* 军人

front line 前线

nurse was that the nurse did not carry a gun.

Nurses in the Philippines had a *particularly tough* time. By late 1941, 88 U.S. Army nurses were stationed there. On December 8 of that year, Japan attacked the islands. It was not a fair match. The Japanese had more men, planes, and ships. Yet the Americans fought bravely to hold out as long as they could.

During the *intense* fighting, the nurses worked hard to do their jobs.

Every day more and more men were brought to the two emergency hospitals. These "hospitals" were nothing more than tents. Even so, there was not room in them for all the wounded men. Some had to be treated out in the open.

Living conditions in the Philippines were *awful*. The water was

---

菲律宾群岛护士的处境尤其艰苦。到1941年年底，88名随军护士被安置在那里。那一年的12月8日，日本袭击了该群岛。这是一场不公平的比赛。日本有更多的士兵、飞机和战舰。但美国人还是英勇地战斗，尽最大可能进行抵抗。

在激烈的战斗中，护士们努力地做她们的工作。

每天都有越来越多的伤员被带到这两处急救医院。这些所谓的"医院"除了帐篷之外什么也没有。即便如此，两处医院还没有足够的地方容下所有的伤员，一些人不得不在户外接受治疗。

菲律宾群岛的生活条件相当糟糕。水极脏，几乎所有的人都患了病。

---

particularly *adv.* 特别地　　　　　　　　　　　　tough *adj.* 艰苦的
intense *adj.* 强烈的　　　　　　　　　　　　　　awful *adj.* 可怕的

filthy. Almost everyone got sick. The Americans *endured* everything from *hookworm* to dengue fever. The nurses had begun their work dressed in starched white uniforms. Before long, they switched to baggy overalls. Food was *scarce*. So rations were cut in half. Then they were cut to three-eighths. People started eating whatever they could find. They ate roots, leaves, monkeys, and pigs.

On March 29, 1942, enemy planes bombed one of the hospitals. A nurse recalled what it was like. "The *sergeant* pulled me under the desk," she said. "The desk was blown into the air, and he and I with it .... Then I fell back to the floor, and the desk landed on top of me."

The sergeant pushed the desk off the nurse. She struggled to her feet and looked around. She was appalled by what she saw. Two nurses had been wounded. More than 100 patients had been hurt

---

美国人忍受着从十二指肠虫到登革热等一切疾病。护士们开始还穿着浆洗过的白大褂工作，不久之后，就改为宽松如袋的罩衫了。食物极为贫乏。因此人均配给被削减到了一半，进而又被减至八分之三。人们开始吃他们所能找到的一切，树根、树叶、猴子和猪。

1942年3月29号，敌军的飞机炸毁了一处医院。一名护士回忆了当时的情形："一名中士把我拽到了桌下"，她说，"桌子被气流掀到了空中，还有他和我……然后我摔了下来，掉到地板上，桌子就落在我的身上。"

那名中士推开了她身上的桌子，她挣扎着站起来，环顾四周。她被眼前的情景吓呆了。两名护士已经受伤；一百多名伤员再次受伤，或者死

---

endure *v.* 忍耐　　　　　　　　　　hookworm *n.* 十二指肠病
scarce *adj.* 缺乏的；不足的　　　　sergeant *n.* 军士；中士

or killed. Some had been blown out of their beds. Severed arms and legs lay all over. Some of these *limbs* were *hanging* from nearby tree branches.

This attack was followed by others. The nurses knew they could do nothing about it. All they could do was care for the wounded and hope for the best.

In early April the Americans suffered a major loss. Thousands were taken prisoner by the Japanese. A few nurses were *captured*. The rest joined *troops* who were fleeing to the island of Corregidor. Hattie Brantley was one of the nurses who fled. She did not want to leave her patients. She did so only when she heard the shouts of Japanese soldiers coming up over the hill toward her. She and other nurses escaped in buses as bombs burst all around them.

亡；一些伤员被炮弹掀翻到了地上；到处是残肢断臂，甚至一些人还悬挂在附近的树枝上。

空袭一次接着一次。护士知道对此她们无能为力。她们所能做的就是照顾受伤士兵，希望做到最好。

四月初，美国人遭受了一次重大失败。数千人被日本人虏为战俘。几名护士也被捕了。其余的加入到了向克莱吉多岛逃亡的军队中。海蒂·布兰特莉是逃亡护士中的一个。她不想离开她的病人。直到她听到翻越山头向她走来的日本人的喊叫声，她才不得已这样做。在四周纷飞的炮火中，她和其他的护士乘巴士逃离。

---

limb *n.* 肢；臂

capture *v.* 捕获

hang *v.* 悬挂

troop *n.* 军队

By April 8 the only part of the Philippines that Americans still held was Corregidor. This island had several tunnels. About 13,000 men and women hid in them. The *tunnels* were safer than tents. But that was little comfort. The tunnels were hot, dark, and noisy. The nurses had to work by *flashlight*. "We were like a bunch of rats in a hole," said nurse Minnie Stubbs. Each day shells blasted the land overhead. "The shelling shook the whole mountain," said Stubbs.

At last, on May 6, the remaining Americans surrendered. Japan now had full control of the Philippines. Sixty-seven nurses became prisoners of war, or *POWs*. They were sent to a prison camp called Santo Tomas. There they stayed for three *grueling* years.

Life as a POW was brutal. The Japanese had strict rules for the prisoners. Anyone who broke them was punished. Many prisoners

到4月8号，菲律宾群岛中只有克莱吉多岛还在美军的掌握中。岛上有几条隧道，大约13,000男人和女人们藏在那里。隧道比帐篷安全，但是一点都不舒服。隧道里又热、又黑，还很吵。护士们必须打手电工作。"我们就像一群洞中的老鼠，"护士米尼·思达布斯说。每天炮弹就在头上方的陆地上爆炸，"炸弹把整个山炸得摇动了。"她说。

最后，在5月6日那一天，剩余的美军投降了。日本现在控制了整个菲律宾群岛。67名护士成了战争中的囚犯，即战俘。他们被送往一个叫作桑托·塔马斯的战俘营。在那里她们度过了残酷的三年。

战俘生活是颇为残酷的。日本人给战俘制定了严厉的规定。任何人破坏了规定，都要受到惩罚。许多战俘因为说谎或试图逃跑而被殴打。

tunnel *n.* 隧道　　　　　flashlight *n.* 手电筒
POW *n.* 战俘　　　　　grueling *adj.* 折磨人的；使人精疲力竭的

were beaten for lying or for trying to escape.

The nurses were sick and hungry when they got to the prison camp. Once there, things got worse. Each day they struggled to get enough to eat. Each person was given a cup of rice twice a day. To eat it, they first had to pick the *bugs* out. Beyond that, the prisoners got nothing. Luckily, they managed to grow some food for themselves. Often they were so *eager* for something green that they ate the leaves of the potatoes as soon as they appeared.

The nurses did what they could for the sick and wounded men who were kept in the prison camp with them. But the nurses had few clean *bandages* and few medicines. They gave patients *aspirin* and vitamin pills. But mostly they offered TLC—tender loving care. They washed faces, held hands, and talked.

当她们到达战俘营时，饥饿的护士们都病着。可是一旦到了那里，情形变得更糟糕。每天他们都在为获得足够的食物做斗争。每个人一天两次只给一碗米饭。要想吃它，还得先挑出里面的臭虫。除此之外，战俘们就什么也得不到了。幸运的是，她们自己设法种了一些粮食。她们常常因为想吃到一点绿色的东西，以至于土豆的叶子刚刚长出来就被吃掉了。

护士们尽其所能帮助和她们在一个战俘营的伤病员们。但是她们几乎没有干净的绷带和药品。她们只能给病人一些阿司匹林和维生素片。但是多数情况下她们只能提供温柔的关爱。她们为病人洗脸，握住他们的手，和他们交谈。

---

bug *n.* 臭虫；小虫
bandage *n.* 绷带

eager *adj.* 渴望的
aspirin *n.* 阿司匹林

The POWs received no news from the outside world. So they had no way of knowing which side was winning the war. Still, they kept their hopes up. Often they climbed trees to look out over the sea. They hoped to see a fleet of American ships. "It was a matter of *faith*," said Hattie Brantley. "We really believed that if we could get through today, help would be there tomorrow."

As time passed, conditions at the camp grew steadily worse. By late 1944 the food ran out. There was no longer even rice for them to eat. The POWs *scrounged* whatever they could. They ate "dogs, frogs, and even rats".

More and more of the prisoners died of *starvation*. But help was on the way. On February 3, 1945, American troops *liberated* the POWs at Santo Tomas. One of the nurses had saved a bottle of

---

战俘们几乎收不到外面世界的任何信息。所以他们也没有办法知道谁赢得了战争的胜利。虽如此，他们仍然保持着希望。他们经常爬上树向海上张望。他们盼望看到美国轮船的影子。"这是一种忠诚，" 海蒂·布兰特莉说，"我们坚信如果我们熬过今天，救援明天就会到来。"

随着时间的推移，战俘营的条件越来越糟。到1944年底，食物用光了。再也没有任何大米可供给他们了。战俘们开始攫取一切可以找到的。他们吃"狗、青蛙，甚至是老鼠"。

越来越多的囚犯死于饥饿。但是救援还在途中。1945年2月3日，美国部队解放了桑托·塔马斯里的战俘。一名护士一直攒着一瓶可乐，为了

---

faith *n.* 信仰；忠诚
starvation *n.* 饿死；挨饿

scrounge *v.* 搜寻；乞讨
liberate *v.* 解放

Coke all this time. To lift morale, she sometimes would take it out of hiding and show it. On this day, she celebrated by finally opening it up. She and all the other ex-POWs stood together and sang "God *Bless* America".

Amazingly, all of the nurses had survived their years in the prison camp. Their *courage* and *kindness* helped other prisoners survive as well. For their heroism in the line of duty, each nurse was promoted. And each received the Bronze Star, one of the highest honors given out by the U.S. Army.

鼓舞士气，有时她会把它从隐藏的地方拿出来给大家看。这一天，为了庆祝，她终于把它打开了。她和所有其他曾经的战俘们站在一起，高唱"上帝保佑美国"。

　　令人惊喜的是，所有护士在几年的战俘生活中都生存下来。她们的勇气和友爱也同样帮助其他战俘存活了下来。由于她们在工作中表现出的英雄气概，每个护士都升了职。并且每一名护士都得到了一枚青铜勋章——美国军队授予的最高荣誉之一。

bless *v.* 祝福；保佑　　　　　　　amazingly *adv.* 令人惊讶地
courage *n.* 勇气　　　　　　　　　kindness *n.* 仁慈

12

Life and Death: The Crash of Flight 242

"**B**end down and *grab* your *ankles*," ordered Sandy Purl. The 81 passengers, who were *buckled* into their seats, did as they were told.

Purl was a flight attendant aboard Southern Airways Flight 242. She wanted the passengers

Southern Airways flight 242 crashed in the yard of a home near New Hope, Georgia.

生死之间

南方航空公司242号航班在位于乔治亚州纽霍普市的一处庭院附近坠毁。

"请弯下腰去抓住自己的脚踝，"桑迪·珀尔命令着飞机上的人。81名已经固定在椅子上的乘客都按照她的吩咐去做。

珀尔是南方航空公司242航班的空中小姐。她想让乘客们做好准备，因为她知道这架DC-9型双引擎喷气式飞机有麻烦了。驾驶舱的挡风玻璃被

---

grab *v.* 抓住；抓取
buckle *v.* 扣紧；扣住

ankle *n.* 踝；脚踝

to be prepared. Purl knew the DC-9 twin engine jet was in trouble. The *windshield* in the cockpit had been *cracked* by *hail*. And moments earlier she had smelled smoke.

As Purl gave instructions to the passengers, she walked back to her seat. Then she clamped on her seat belt. She *braced* herself for a crash landing.

It was April 4, 1977. Purl was one of a four-person crew. The others were Captain William McKenzie, his copilot Lyman Keele, and flight attendant Cathy Lemoine. For the past two days, these four men and women had worked as a team on a series of short flights. They had just two hops left. First they were to fly from Huntsville, Alabama, to Atlanta, Georgia. Then they would continue on to New Orleans, Louisiana. The distance from Huntsville to Atlanta was only 150 miles. It was on this short flight, however, that things went wrong.

冰雹打裂；片刻前她还闻到了烟的味道。

珀尔要求乘客按照她的吩咐去做的时候，她退回到自己的座位上。并扣好安全带，强打精神为飞机的强行着陆做着准备。

飞机出现故障的时候是1977年4月4日。珀尔所在的机组有四名乘务员，另外三人是机长威廉·麦肯济、副驾驶莱曼·基勒以及另一名空姐凯茜·莱蒙恩。在头两天，他们四个人已经做了一系列的短途飞行，现在只剩下两班短途飞行任务。开始他们打算从阿拉巴玛州的亨特斯维尔飞到乔治亚州的亚特兰大市，然后他们接着飞到路易斯安那州的新奥尔良市。亨特斯维尔到亚特兰大的距离只有150英里，然而就是在这次短途飞行中灾难降临了。

---

windshield *n.* 挡风玻璃

hail *n.* 冰雹

crack *v.* 破裂

brace *v.* 支撑；振作起来

The DC-9 had climbed to 17,000 feet. A storm of rain and heavy hail began to batter the plane. High winds made the jet bounce wildly. Purl heard three loud bangs in the left engine. The cabin lights *flickered* and went out. A few moments later, the lights came back on again. Purl picked up her *microphone*. She knew she needed to calm the passengers. "Keep your seat belts securely fastened," she said *reassuringly*. "There's nothing to be alarmed about. Relax. We should be out of the storm shortly."

But suddenly Purl smelled smoke. That's when she realized the plane was in serious trouble. *Unbuckling* her seat belt, she walked to the passengers who were sitting next to the exit windows. She talked softly to them. She had to be sure they knew what to do if the plane made a crash landing.

　　当这架DC-9型飞机爬升到一万七千英尺高空的时候，一场暴风雨夹杂着大块的冰雹开始向它袭来，疾风吹得飞机猛烈地抖动。珀尔听到左侧引擎发出三声"砰"的撞击声音，随之机舱的灯闪了几下就熄灭了，片刻以后，这些灯自己又亮了起来。珀尔知道她应该让乘客们镇静下来，她拿起麦克风心平气和地说："请各位把座位上的安全带都系好。大家不必惊慌，请放松。我们很快就会冲出这片风暴。"

　　可是珀尔忽然闻到了一股烟味儿，此时她意识到飞机真的有大麻烦了。她解开座位上的安全带走到靠着安全出口窗户附近的乘客身旁，轻声嘱咐他们。她要让他们知道一旦飞机紧急降落应该采取什么样的措施。

---

flicker *v.* 使闪烁
reassuringly *adv.* 安慰地；鼓励地

microphone *n.* 麦克风
unbuckle *v.* 解开

Purl didn't know it, but the loud noises she'd heard meant that the left engine had died. Soon the right engine stopped working as well. This was the first time such a thing had happened to a DC-9. In 112 million hours of flying time, no DC-9 engine had ever failed in a *rainstorm*. But in this case, huge amounts of rain and hail had been *sucked* into the engines. Both of them *malfunctioned* at almost the same instant.

While Sandy Purl tried to keep the passengers calm, Captain McKenzie struggled to land the plane safely. He knew he'd never make it to the airport in Atlanta. He couldn't even make it to Dobbins Air Force base just 15 miles away. In fact, McKenzie knew he couldn't make it to any airport. He had to land the plane *right away*. But where?

珀尔并不知道飞机出了什么故障，但是传到耳朵里来的巨大噪音表明左侧的引擎已经坏掉了。很快，右侧的引擎也停止了工作。对于DC-9来说，以前从来没有出现过这样的故障。在总共一亿一千二百万个小时飞行中，DC-9的引擎没有过在暴风雨中失灵的先例。但是这一次引擎吸进了大量的雨水和冰雹，这使得两侧的引擎几乎在一瞬间都出现了故障。

就在珀尔努力让乘客保持平静的同时，麦肯济机长正竭尽全力让飞机平安着陆。他知道飞机不可能飞到亚特兰大的机场了，他甚至无法驾驶飞机赶到就在15英里以外的多宾斯空军基地。麦肯济明白他不可能赶到任何一座机场了，飞机必须马上就降落。但是，降落在哪里呢？

---

rainstorm *n.* 暴风雨

malfunction *v.* 发生故障

suck *v.* 吸吮；吸进

right away 立刻

His best chance seemed to be Route 92 near New Hope, Georgia. He aimed the plane for this *two-lane* highway. As the plane descended, its wings clipped trees, road signs, and telephone poles. The jet smashed into three cars. It took the roof off a local *grocery* store. Then, as it veered into the woods, it *erupted* in a ball of flames. It finally stopped moving 200 yards from the road.

Ruby Shipp, who lived across the highway, heard the crash. At first she thought it was thunder. "I thought, Lord, it's the *tornado* they were talking about on the television," she said. "I looked out and it was a solid black cloud of smoke. But I saw it was not a tornado. It was a plane on fire."

The crash killed nine people on the ground. It also killed many

---

对于机长来说最佳选择看来就是位于乔治亚州纽霍普市的92号公路。他驾驶飞机朝着这条有两条车道的高速公路飞去。飞机降落的时候，机翼削掉了树枝、路标以及电话线杆子。这架喷气式飞机撞碎了三辆汽车；还把当地一家食品杂货店的房顶掀翻。然后它调转方向朝着树林冲了进去，同时一团火球从飞机中喷射出来。最后飞机在距离公路200码的地方停了下来。

住在高速公路对面的鲁比·茜普听到了飞机坠毁的声音。起初她以为是打雷的声音。"当时我想，上帝，这就是他们在电视上经常提到的龙卷风吧，"她说，"我看见了黑色的柱状烟云。但是我发现那并不是龙卷风，而是飞机着火了。"

坠落的飞机撞死了九个地面上的人。飞机上面的很多人失去了生命，

---

two-lane 双车道
erupt *v.* 爆发；喷发

grocery *n.* 食品杂货店
tornado *n.* 龙卷风

people on board. But not everyone on the plane died. Purl survived the crash in relatively good shape. When the plane stopped, however, she saw nothing but a wall of flames ahead of her. She tried to get out the back exit. But the door wouldn't open.

Purl feared she was trapped. She knew poison fumes from the fire would kill her in less than a minute. So she *shielded* her face with her arm and scrambled for the front exit. Fortunately, it was open and she was able to hop out onto the ground.

As she moved away from the *wreckage*, she looked back. The part of the plane where she had been sitting suddenly exploded. Pieces of metal went flying through the air. She could smell burning jet fuel as well as burning flesh.

As the shock of the crash began to *wear off*, Purl's mind turned to the passengers. She realized some of them might still be *alive*.

但是仍然有幸存者。珀尔就活了下来而且没有受太重的伤。然而当飞机停下来的时候，除了面前的一堵火墙她什么都看不见了。她试图从后面的出口逃出去，但是那个门打不开了。

珀尔担心她困在里面出不来，她知道大火燃烧时产生的有毒气体不出一分钟就会毒死她，因此她用手臂捂住脸爬向前门。幸运的是前门打开了，她跳到了地面上。

当离开飞机残骸的时候她回头看了一眼，就在这时她刚刚还坐着的地方发生了爆炸。一片片的金属飞到了空中。她闻到了火烧肉的味道和飞机燃料的味道。

等到头脑中的惊骇稍稍减退一些，珀尔的注意力就集中到了乘客的身上。她意识到也许有一些乘客还活着。珀尔看到了一名被严重烧伤的乘客

---

shield *v.* 挡开；避开
wear off 逐渐消失

wreckage *n.* 残骸
alive *adj.* 活着的

She saw one badly burned man lying on the ground. She pulled him away from the flames. After getting him to the safety of the road, Purl rushed back to the burning wreckage. She saw another passenger with his suit on fire. Purl knocked him to the ground, rolling him over and over until she had *snuffed out* the flames.

By this time, rescue workers were beginning to arrive. One of them tried to lead Purl away from the crash site. But she protested and raced back to the plane to look for more survivors. The only thought she had was what she had learned in her safety training: "You are *responsible* for your passengers."

As Purl picked through the sheets of hot metal, she *enlisted* several other surviving passengers to help her. She got *bystanders* to cover the people who were burned. And she told others how to care for those in shock.

躺在地上，她把那个人从火中拖了出来，放到了公路上安全的地带，而后又急匆匆返回到还在着火的飞机残骸旁。她看到另一名乘客的衣服已经着火，就把他放倒在地上，让他滚来滚去，一直到身上的火被扑灭。

此时，营救人员已经开始纷纷到达。其中一个人想要带珀尔离开出事的地点，但是她表示反对，又跑了回去寻找更多的幸存者。此时她大脑中的唯一的想法就是曾经在安全训练中学到的教诲："你要对你的乘客负责。"

珀尔在烫手的铁片中搜寻的时候，她得到了其他许多幸存者的帮助。她请求周围的旁观者把烧坏的乘客盖上，然后又告诉他们如何照料受到惊吓的乘客。

snuff out 扼杀；消灭
enlist v. 赢得……支持

responsible adj. 负责的
bystander n. 旁观者

During this time, Purl never noticed how badly her own feet were cut. In fact, she was functioning in a daze. Her mind could not *absorb* the *horror*. At one point she asked an *ambulance* nurse, "Am I alive?" The nurse said yes. But Purl only half believed her. This nurse wanted Purl to go to the hospital with the other survivors, but Purl refused. She wanted to find the rest of the crew.

Then Purl spotted the remains of the cockpit. Walking over to it, she saw the bodies of Captain McKenzie and copilot Keele. At that point, there was little left for her to do.

In all, the crash of Southern Airways Flight 242 killed 63 people. But there was some good news for Purl. Flight attendant Cathy Lemoine survived. She, too, helped to save some of the passengers. Thanks in part to these women's courage and sense of duty, 20 passengers survived the crash.

在此期间，珀尔根本没有注意到她脚上的伤势有多严重。事实上她一直是在眩晕中抢救乘客的，她的意识里根本没有恐惧的概念。某一片刻她问一名救护车上的护士："我是不是还活着？"护士给了她肯定的回答，但是她仍然半信半疑。这名护士想要珀尔和其他的幸存者一起去医院，但是她拒绝了，她想要留下来继续寻找剩下的机组人员。

然后珀尔找到了驾驶员座舱的残骸。走到残骸上面的时候，她发现了麦肯济机长和副驾驶员基勒的尸体。当时，珀尔感觉到已经没有任何希望了。

此次南方航空公司242号航班的空难一共造成了63人死亡。但是对于珀尔来说还是有一些值得欣慰的消息——另一名空中小姐凯茜·莱蒙恩也逃过了一劫。当时她也帮助挽救了一些乘客的生命。从某种角度说，因为有了两名女子的勇气和责任感，20名乘客才能得以从飞机坠毁中幸免于难。

---

absorb *v.* 使……全神贯注

ambulance *n.* 救护车

horror *n.* 恐惧

13

Courage at Knifepoint

"Take me to Las Vegas!" With these words, a 17-year-old *hijacker* pressed a knife to Lilia Rios's *throat*.

Lilia Rios had every right to expect a routine day. She drove a bus for the *Desert* Sands Unified School District in Indio, California. Rios had been driving for 17 years. She had more

School bus driver Lilia Rios gets a hug and some roses from one of the students who was on her bus when it was hijacked.

刀尖勇气

校车司机莉丽娅·里约斯与一名学生拥抱，并接受她的玫瑰花。当劫持发生的时候，这个孩子就在她的车上。

"把我送到拉斯维加斯！"说着这些话，一个17岁的劫持者将一把尖刀压在了莉丽娅·里约斯的喉咙上。

莉丽娅·里约斯有足够的理由期待常规的一天。她为加利福尼亚州荒漠之沙联合学校校区开车。里约斯有17年的开车史。她比其他任何一个司机都有经验。

---

hijacker *n.* 抢劫者
desert *n.* 沙漠

throat *n.* 喉咙

experience than any of the other drivers.

On October 1, 1996, Lilia Rios began her 3 P.M. school bus run. She picked up 90 students at the Roosevelt *Elementary School*. Her first stop was at King Street and Bliss Avenue. Then she stopped at the corner of Civic Center Drive and Towne Street. After students got off at that stop, only 31 students were still on board. The students were quite young. Most of them were in first or second grade.

Just as Rios was about to close the door, a 17-year-old stranger *appeared*. He pushed his way onto the bus. Then he *pulled out* a 12-inch knife. He ordered Rios to drive him to *Las Vegas*.

When Rios hesitated, he hissed, "Lady, do you want me to kill you?" He then added that he would kill the children if she didn't do exactly what he wanted.

1996年10月1日，莉丽娅·里约斯在下午3点开始跑车。她在罗斯福小学接了90名学生。她的第一站是金大街和布里斯大道。接着她到斯维克中心街和汤尼大街拐角处停靠。到了这一站学生下车后，只有31名学生还在车上。学生们都很小。多数都是一二年级。

就在里约斯关车门的那一刹那，一个17岁的陌生人出现了。他挤上了车，然后抽出了一把12英寸的刀。他命令里约斯把他送到拉斯维加斯。

当里约斯犹豫的时候，他嘘了一声，说："女士，你想让我杀了你吗？"接着他又说，要是她不按照他说的做，他将杀掉车上的孩子。

---

elementary school 小学
pull out 拔出

appear v. 出现
Las Vegas 拉斯维加斯

Rios closed the door of the bus and began to drive. As she did so, she *glanced* in the *rearview mirror*. She could see the frightened faces of the young children behind her. Some of them were crying and screaming.

Then Rios looked up at the hijacker. "I told myself, 'He's crazy,'" recalled Rios. "'He's going to kill me and the children.'"

But Rios was determined not to let that happen. She felt responsible for every single child on her bus. "I love those kids," she said later. "They are like my own."

So Rios, a mother of four, formed her own plan. She *sensed* that the hijacker was nervous. In fact, he seemed just as scared as she was. "I'm not going to listen [to him]," she thought to herself. "I'm not going to play it his way." As they drove, Rios began talking back

---

里约斯关上了车门开始开车。就在她这样做的时候，她瞥了一下后视镜，看到的是后面一张张被吓坏的孩子的脸。一些孩子还在哭喊尖叫。

里约斯抬头看了看劫持者。"我告诉我自己：'他一定是疯了，他会杀了我和孩子们的。'"里约斯回忆时说。

但是里约斯决定不让这种事情发生。她觉得她应该为车上的每一个孩子负责。后来她说："我爱那些孩子，他们就像我自己的孩子一样。"

所以里约斯，一个四个孩子的母亲，开始制定她自己的计划。她感觉劫持者很紧张。事实上，他似乎是和她一样害怕。她想："我不准备听（他的话），我不能按照他的想法进行。"她一边开车，一边回应他的话。当劫持者向她喊的时候，她就用更大的声音回复他。而且可以看出他

---

glance *v.* 扫视；瞥见

sense *v.* 感觉

rearview mirror 后视镜

to him. When he yelled at her, she yelled back louder. She could see him getting *rattled*. She could feel herself slowly gaining the upper hand. Still, he kept pressing the *blade* of his knife against her throat.

Meanwhile, the children on the bus continued to scream. One of them was third-grader Laura Campos. At one point Rios passed a bus stop. Campos *yelled out* the window to people standing there. The people heard Campos's cries and dialed 911. Neither Rios nor the hijacker knew it, but the police would soon be on their way.

After several minutes, the hijacker *demanded* that Rios give him money for gas. She pointed out that it would take a lot of fuel to get all the way to Las Vegas. She told him she didn't have enough money for that. But Rios said she knew where she could get some gas for free. All she had to do was stop at the Desert Sands bus yard. That's where the school buses always filled their tanks. Without

---

变得很恼火。并能够感觉到自己正在赢得上风。虽然他仍然用刀抵着自己的喉咙。

同时，车上的孩子继续尖叫。其中的一个是三年级的劳拉·坎波斯。有那么一瞬间，里约斯路过了一个汽车站。坎波斯冲着站在窗外的人群大叫。人们听到了她的喊声并且拨打了911。里约斯和劫持者都不知道此事，但是警察将很快出现在他们的道路上。

几分钟之后，劫持者命令里约斯给他钱加油。但里约斯说要去拉斯维加斯需要很多燃料，并且她没有足够的钱。但是里约斯说她知道哪里可以得到免费的汽油。她必须做的就是停到荒漠之沙停车场。那就是校车加油

---

rattle *v.* 使生气
yell out 大声叫喊

blade *n.* 刀片
demand *v.* 要求

giving the hijacker time to say no, Rios turned the bus away from the freeway and headed for the bus yard.

When she pulled the bus into the yard, however, the hijacker grew angry. He started screaming. Rios screamed back at him. She stopped the bus, opened the door, and turned to face her captor.

Then, suddenly, Rios took a wild chance. She reached out and *grabbed* at the knife. As she *wrestled* for control of it, the children in the bus screamed in terror. Rios and the young man *tumbled* out of the bus. Rios cried out for help. Two *mechanics* in the yard heard her. "Please help me," she pleaded. "He has a knife. He wants to kill me."

The hijacker pulled the knife away from Rios. He scrambled to his feet and ran away.

Just then, the police arrived. They caught the hijacker as he fled.

的地方。没给劫持者时间说不，里约斯掉转车头离开高速公路，直奔校园停车场。

然而正当她把车开进了场院内时，劫持者暴怒了。他开始尖叫，里约斯也回应尖叫。她停了车，开了车门，转脸朝向她的俘虏。

突然间，里约斯大胆地冒险，伸出手抓住了刀。正当她使劲想控制它时，车上的孩子们惊恐地大喊。里约斯和年轻人跌出了车外，并大喊求救。场院中的两个修理工听到她的喊声。"救命！"她祈求道，"他有刀，他想杀我。"

劫持者从里约斯的手中拽出了刀，爬起来跑了。
就在那时，警察赶到了。他们在劫持者逃离过程中抓住了他。那个年轻人被指控和几起案件有关，包括用致命武器袭击案和绑架案。

---

grab *v.* 攫取；抓取
tumble *v.* 跌倒；摔倒

wrestle *v.* 使劲；全力解决
mechanic *n.* 技工

The young man was charged with several crimes, including assault with a deadly weapon and kidnapping.

For Lilia Rios and the children on the bus, the hijacking had a happy ending. Thanks to Rios, they were all safe. "I'm no hero," said Rios modestly. "I just did my job. The children are fine, and that's what matters. I kept thinking of the kids."

Two weeks later, Lilia Rios was honored by other bus drivers and the school district. She was given flowers and a *plaque*. Third-grader Laura Campos also was honored. It was her screaming out the bus window that brought the police to the scene.

Some bus drivers *urged* Rios to begin driving a different bus route. They thought a change of *scenery* might help her forget that knife at her throat. But Lilia Rios said no. She wanted to be there for the kids who had also *lived through* the terror. "When I get on the bus," Lilia Rios said, "I'm going to tell them that I love them."

对于莉丽娅·里约斯和车上的孩子们来说，这次劫持案结果让人高兴。多亏了里约斯，所有人都保证了安全。"我不是英雄，"里约斯谦虚地说。"我只是做了我的工作。孩子们一切都好，那是最重要的。我始终都在想着孩子们。"

两周后，里约斯被其他校车司机和学校授予荣誉。她得到了鲜花和一块纪念匾。三年级的劳拉·坎波斯同样得到奖励。就是由于她向窗外大声求救才把警察带到现场。

一些校车司机劝里约斯换一条线路。他们认为换一换周围的景色可以帮助她忘记喉咙上的尖刀。但是莉丽娅·里约斯不同意。她想和那些同样经历了恐怖事件的孩子们在一起。莉丽娅·里约斯说："当我上车的时候，我要告诉他们我爱他们。"

---

plaque *n.* 匾
scenery *n.* 景色；风景

urge *v.* 力劝；敦促
live through 度过；经历过

14

Rescue Mission

"**G**et us out of here!" pleaded a voice on the radio. "For God's *sake*, get us out!" The call came from the leader of 12 American soldiers trapped inside Cambodia. These soldiers were in big trouble. A large force of enemy troops had *surrounded* them. Four of the soldiers were already dead. All of the

U.S. Marines on duty in Vietnam

独闯龙潭

美国海军陆战队在越南执行任务

"救我们出去！"无线电中传来一阵阵呼救的声音，"看在上帝的面子上，把我们救出去！"呼救人是有12名成员的美国士兵小分队的队长，他们失陷于柬埔寨。小分队的士兵遇到了麻烦，他们被大批敌军包围，4名队员已经阵亡，剩下的8个人也都受了伤。

---

sake *n.* 目的；理由

surround *v.* 包围

remaining eight were wounded.

It was May 2, 1968. America was at war in Vietnam. Cambodia was not part of the war. But enemy troops from North Vietnam often traveled through Cambodia. So U.S. troops sometimes went there, too, *in order to* spy on the enemy. That's what the 12 Americans had been doing. But 30 miles inside Cambodia, they had been trapped. Could anyone save them?

Sergeant Roy Benavidez was at Loc Ninh in Vietnam when the distress call came in. He could hear the sound of gunfire over the *airwaves*. "There was so much shooting," he said, "it sounded like a popcorn machine."

Three helicopters were sent to *rescue* the stranded men. But the choppers couldn't land. The enemy blasted them every time they

---

这是1968年的5月2日，美国和越南正在进行战争。当时柬埔寨并没有卷入战争，但是越南的军队经常穿越柬埔寨，因此美国的部队有时候也去那里进行侦察活动。12名士兵此次正是要执行这样的行动，但是在进入柬埔寨30英里的时候他们被包围了，他们能生还么？

令人担忧的求救信号传来的时候，罗伊·班纳维德兹中士正在越南的禄宁。他都能听到话筒里面炮火的声音，他说："这么密集的枪声，听起来就像爆米花机。"

三架直升机被派往柬埔寨营救险境中的士兵。但是直升机却无法着陆，只要他们一靠近，敌人的炮火就会向他们射来。最后飞行员们不得不

---

in order to 为了

airwaves n. 无线电波

sergeant n. 军士；中士

rescue v. 营救

came close. At last, the pilots flew back to Loc Ninh. Benavidez ran to the first chopper. A wounded crewman fell out and landed in his arms. A few moments later, the man died.

Soon another chopper was sent to try to rescue the Americans. Benavidez grabbed his rifle and climbed on board. No one ordered him to go. But he knew his fellow soldiers were in trouble. He wanted to help. He later said, "When I got on that *copter*, little did I know we were going to spend six hours in hell."

When this helicopter neared the trouble spot, the enemy was still firing away. It was impossible to get near the wounded men. The pilot flew to within 75 yards. But he could not get any closer than that. With the chopper *hovering* 10 feet off the ground, Benavidez made his move. He jumped out onto the ground. Then, all alone, he

---

飞回禄宁。班纳维德兹奔向飞机，此时一名受伤的机组乘务员从飞机上掉了下来压在自己的胳膊上，没过多久就死掉了。

很快，另一架直升机被派出去营救被围困的士兵。这一次，班纳维德兹抓过自己的步枪爬上了飞机。并没有人命令他这样做，但是他知道他的战友正在危难之中，他要去帮助他们。他后来说："当我登上飞机的时候，我万万没有想到会在地狱般的困境中度过6个小时。"

当班纳维德兹的直升机抵达营救地点的时候，敌人的火力仍不停地射击，他们根本不可能接近那些伤员。飞机在距离伤员们75码远的10英尺上空盘旋，再也无法靠近。这时候，班纳维德兹自己行动了。他跳到地面上，然后一个人穿过战场朝着受伤的战友跑去。

---

copter *n.* 直升机　　　　　　　　　　　　　hover *v.* 徘徊；盘旋

dashed through a field toward the wounded men.

Enemy soldiers saw him. They opened fire. Bullets flew all around him. They hit him in the head, the face, and the right leg. Several times Benavidez fell down. But each time he scrambled to his feet and kept running. "When you're shot," he said, "you feel a burning pain like you've been touched with a hot metal. The fear that you experience is worse—and that's what keeps you going."

At last Benavidez reached the stranded troops. He used a *smoke grenade* to mark a place where the chopper could land. Then he turned to the wounded men. He told them they had to shoot back at the enemy as hard and fast as they could. That would *distract* the enemy long enough to let the helicopter *fly in*.

The plan worked. With the Americans training their fire on the enemy, the pilot managed to get to the spot Benavidez had marked.

敌军士兵发现了他，并一起向他开火。子弹在他身旁飞过，他的头、脸和右腿都被子弹击中。好几次班纳维德兹摔倒在地上，但每次他都爬起来然后接着向前跑。"当中枪的时候，"他说，"你会感觉像触摸一块烫人的金属一样。而恐惧更是让人难以忍受，这也是为什么你能不停地跑的原因。"

终于，班纳维德兹来到了受伤战友的身旁。他用烟雾手榴弹标明一块地方以便于直升机降落。然后他转向等待援救的伤员，并告诉他们必须立即狠狠地向敌人还击，这样才能吸引敌人的火力好让飞机飞进来。

这个计划果然奏效了。趁着美国兵和敌人对射的空隙飞行员努力地把飞机降落在班纳维德兹用烟雾手榴弹标出的地方。之后班纳维德兹不顾自

---

dash *v.* 飞奔　　　　　　　　　　　smoke grenade　烟雾弹

distract *v.* 转移；分心　　　　　　　fly in　降落

Then Benavidez picked up one of the wounded men. *Ignoring* the pain of his own wounds, he carried the man to the chopper. Then he ran back for the next man. He managed to get four of the wounded men on board.

But before Benavidez could do anything more, he was hit in the back and *stomach*. He fell to the ground. As he looked up, he saw the helicopter get hit, too. It burst into flames. Benavidez struggled to his feet. He raced to the wreck. The pilot and two of the wounded soldiers were dead. Benavidez pulled the other men out of the fire. He gathered them into a circle with the four other wounded soldiers. The *situation* looked *hopeless*. It seemed the enemy could overrun them at any time.

Benavidez used his radio to call for help. Soon helicopters arrived and began shooting at the enemy. Benavidez kept his little

---

己的伤痛，抱起一名伤员把他放到了飞机上。然后他又跑回去，一共帮助四名伤员登上飞机。

但是正当班纳维德兹准备去救第五个人的时候，一颗子弹射中了他的后背，并且射伤了他的胃，他倒在了地上。他抬起头，看到飞机也被击中并且着起火来。飞行员和两名刚刚被送上去的伤员被打死了。班纳维德兹朝着飞机残骸奔过去，把另外两名幸存的战友救了下来，又把他们和其余四名没有上飞机的伤员聚拢到一起。形势看起来没有希望了，敌人随时会消灭他们。

班纳维德兹用无线电向总部请求支援。很快直升机飞来了并且开始向敌军扫射。班纳维德兹也率领他的伤员小分队朝敌人开火。与此同时，

---

ignore *v.* 忽视；忽略
situation *n.* 情况；形式

stomach *n.* 胃
hopeless *adj.* 绝望的

group firing away too. Meanwhile, he did his best to treat the men's wounds. He also tried to care for his own wounds. Still, blood from his head *trickled* into his eyes. That made it hard for him to see. As he tended to one of his men, a bullet struck him in the thigh. It was another of the 36 wounds that Roy Benavidez would suffer before the day was over.

More choppers came to get the men out. But enemy fire knocked most of them out of the sky. At last, after several hours, one got close enough to land. Once more, Benavidez began to drag wounded soldiers to the chopper. But his *ordeal* was not over yet.

As he went to pick up one man, an enemy soldier charged at him. The enemy hit him over the head with the *butt* of a rifle. Benavidez wheeled around. He saw that the soldier was about to *stab* him with his bayonet. Desperately, Benavidez reached for the blade. As

---

他尽自己最大的努力来处置伤员和自己的伤口。血从头上一直流淌到他的眼睛里，以至于他几乎看不清周围的情形。正当他全力处理一名战友的时候，一颗子弹击中了他的大腿。这是天黑前罗伊·班纳维德兹所受的36处伤口中的又一处伤。

更多的飞机赶来援救他们，但是大多数都被敌军的炮火击落了下来。几个小时以后，一架飞机终于接近了等待救援的伤员们。班纳维德兹再一次开始往飞机上拖这些受伤的士兵。但是此时，严酷的考验又向他袭来。

就当他伸手去扶地上伤员的时候，一名敌军向他冲了过来，并且用枪托猛击他的头部。班纳维德兹转过身来，他看到敌人正准备用刺刀刺他，他伸手拼命地抓住了刀刃。刺刀割进了他的肌肉，但是没能伤到他的身

---

trickle *v.* 流出；滴；淌

butt *n.* 枪托；枪柄

ordeal *n.* 严峻考验

stab *v.* 刺

he grabbed it, the bayonet cut through his hand. But at least that stopped the thrust. Then Benavidez took out his own knife and killed the soldier.

Benavidez *stumbled* back to the helicopter. He was bleeding heavily from his many wounds. Yet he helped load the rest of the wounded men onto the chopper. He even shot down two more enemy soldiers as they charged toward him.

At last, when all the other men were on board, Benavidez allowed himself to be pulled into the chopper. He *collapsed* on the floor. His *intestines* were *spilling out* of a wound in his stomach. He had to use his hands to hold them in.

With enemy bullets still flying, the chopper took off. Luckily, the bullets did not hit anything vital. The group made it back to Loc Ninh safely.

体。之后，他抽出自己的刀捅进了敌人的身体。

班纳维德兹跌跌撞撞地走向飞机，血顺着身上多处伤口不停地往外流淌着。即使这样，他还是帮助剩下的几名伤员爬上了飞机，甚至还转身击毙了两名扑上来的敌人。

终于，看到所有的伤员都上了飞机，班纳维德兹才让自己也爬上去。他一登上飞机就一头栽倒在地面上，肠子顺着胃部的伤口流了出来，他不得不用手托着它们。

飞机在呼啸的子弹声中离开。幸运的是这次飞机没有受到严重的损害，机上人员得以安全返回禄宁。

---

stumble v. 蹒跚；东倒西歪地走
intestine n. 肠；内脏

collapse v. 倒坍
spill out 溢出

By then, Benavidez had lost a huge amount of blood. He had no strength left. He could not move or speak. The first doctor who looked at him thought he was dead. To show he was not, Benavidez did the only thing he could manage. He *spit* in the doctor's face.

It took Benavidez a long time to recover from his wounds. His actions won him the nation's highest medal. This was the Congressional Medal of Honor. His award read in part, "For *conspicuous gallantry* ... above and beyond the call of duty."

A Mexican American, Benavidez felt a great sense of loyalty towards the United States. "I'm proud to be an American," he said. "I'm proud to serve my country—serve it well. I'm proud of being rewarded for a job well done."

Still, Benavidez did not think of himself as a hero. Once someone told him that his one-man battle was *extraordinary*. "No," replied Roy Benavidez. "That's duty."

此时的班纳维德兹由于失血过多，已经没有任何力气。他一动不动，也说不出话。开始为他治病的医生看到他后以为他已经死了。为了表明自己还活着，班纳维德兹用尽了自己最后一点力气做了一件事情——朝着那名医生的脸上吐了一口水。

很长时间以后，班纳维德兹的伤情才得以康复。他的英勇行为为他赢得了美国最高级别的奖项——国家荣誉勋章。他的勋章也可以表明他"异乎寻常的英勇……远远超出了一名士兵的范畴。"

作为一名墨西哥裔美国人，班纳维德兹对美利坚合众国有着很深的忠诚感。他说："我为我是美国人感到骄傲；我为我能做出贡献，能全心全意地为国家服务骄傲；我也为工作出色获得奖赏而骄傲。"

然而，班纳维德兹并没有把他自己当作英雄。一次有人对他说他一个人的战斗是如此英勇的时候，罗伊·班纳维德兹回答说："不，那只是我的职责所在。"

---

spit *v.* 吐；吐出

gallantry *n.* 勇敢

conspicuous *adj.* 显著的

extraordinary *adj.* 非凡的；惊人的

15

Fallen Heroes

It was just an empty building. The 80-year-old warehouse in the city of *Worcester*, Massachusetts had not been used for a long time. But the building's five floors were not always *deserted*. *Homeless* people who had no other place to stay often *slipped* into the warehouse to get out of the cold.

Firefighters stand at the scene as the Worcester Cold Storage and Warehouse continues to burn. Six firefighters died in the blaze.

出生入死

消防员站在伍斯特的冷藏存储仓库失火现场。六名消防员在此次大火中丧生。

这是一座空的建筑物。这座80岁的仓储大楼坐落在马萨诸塞州伍斯特市，已经好久没有人使用它了。但是这座五层的大楼并非总是荒废的。无家可归而又别无去处的人经常溜进去躲避寒冷的天气。有时候这些人整晚都待在那里。

Worcester *n.* 伍斯特（城市）
homeless *adj.* 无家可归的

deserted *adj.* 荒芜的；被遗弃的
slip *v.* 溜进；溜走

Sometimes these people stayed all night.

That was the case on December 3, 1999. A man and a woman were staying on the second floor of the warehouse. In fact, they had been living there for months. On this night, though, the couple apparently had a fight. Police believe they accidentally *tipped over* a lighted candle. The flame spread to some clothes and papers. The couple tried to put out the growing fire. When they couldn't, they *panicked* and *ran away*. They did not ring any fire *alarms*. And they told no one that the building was now empty.

Worcester firefighters were called to the blaze just after six o'clock in the evening. About 25 of them went into the warehouse. They went in to fight the fire. But they were also looking to see if anyone was inside. The firefighters knew that homeless people used

---

　　事件发生在1999年12月3日。一名男子和一名女子待在这座仓储大楼的第二层。实际上他们已经住在这里有几个月了。而当天晚上，很明显这两个人吵架了。警察确信他们不小心打翻了照明用的蜡烛，火点燃了一些衣服和纸张。他们两个想要扑灭蔓延起来的火势，但是没有办到，于是惊慌失措地跑掉了。他们没有发出任何救火的警报也没有告诉任何人这座大楼已经是空的了。

　　伍斯特的消防队员在傍晚6点接到火警的命令然后赶往现场。大约有25名队员冲进了仓储大楼。他们要进去扑灭大火，同时也搜寻一下里面是否有人。队员们知道无家可归的人经常把这里当作自己的避难所，所以想

---

tip over 使翻倒
run away 逃跑

panick *v.* 恐慌
alarm *n.* 警报

the warehouse as a shelter. They wanted to save anyone who might be trapped there.

When they got inside, they found the second, third, and fourth floors *engulfed* in flames. Still, the fire looked manageable at first. Then, without warning, it *flared up*. The heat, smoke, and flames were so *fearsome* that Fire Chief Michael McNamee called for extra help.

Ten more firefighters came to the warehouse. By then the fire had grown even worse. The old brick warehouse was a firetrap. It was a maze of dark, smoky rooms. None of these rooms had windows. The lack of windows meant that the fire's heat was trapped inside. Large areas of open space helped to spread the fire. Also, the ceiling and walls had cork *insulation*. The burning cork added to the smoke. "You

---

要救出困在里面的人。

当他们进到楼里面的时候，发现火势已经把二楼、三楼和四楼笼罩住。开始火势是可以控制住的。然而，大火在没有任何征兆的情况下突然发怒，热浪、浓烟以及火焰异常恐怖地扑来，以至于消防队长麦克尔·麦克纳米不得不要求增派人手。

另外十名消防队员赶到了仓储大楼。此时火势已经变得更加凶猛。这座老式的砖块建造的大楼是极容易失火、又很难逃离的建筑物，楼里面的房间都没有窗户。没有窗户就意味着热量难以散发，大块的开阔地带更利于火势的蔓延。而且天花板和墙壁都是软木绝缘体，燃烧的软木和浓烟掺

---

engulf *v.* 吞没
fearsome *adj.* 可怕的

flare up 突然燃烧
insulation *n.* 绝缘

couldn't see six inches in front of your face," said McNamee.

All fires are hard to fight. But a fire in an *abandoned* building is especially difficult. That is because such buildings are often in bad shape. People come in and *rip out* the *plumbing* and wiring. They sell the materials for *scrap*. But that leaves holes in the floors and walls. Sometimes steps in the stairways are missing. Walking through such a place can be very dangerous. The firefighters had to walk through it in the dark while almost blind from the smoke. They knew they were risking their lives with every step they took.

Soon Fire Chief McNamee realized that his firefighters faced a nearly hopeless task. The fire was out of control. So he told everyone to get out of the building. Then he ordered a head count. By then it was about 7:30 P.M.. McNamee wanted to make sure all his people

---

杂在一起。"你根本无法看到面前六英寸远的物体。"麦克纳米说。

　　所有的火灾都是很难救的，但是扑灭一座废弃大楼里面的大火尤其困难。因为这样的建筑结构已经是惨不忍睹——经常有人拔出里面的管道或者电线，他们把这些东西当作废品卖掉，所以地板上、墙壁上已是千疮百孔。有时候楼梯间的台阶已经不见了，在这样的环境里穿行是十分危险的。由于烟雾笼罩了一切可见的东西，消防队员不得不摸索着在楼道里穿行。他们知道每迈出一步都可能有丧命的危险。

　　很快麦克纳米意识到他们面临着无法完成的任务，大火已经失去控制。所以他让消防队员们撤出大楼。然后命令手下统计一下人数。此时大约是晚上7点30分，麦克纳米希望队员都能够平安撤出来。但是，有人没

---

abandoned *adj.* 被抛弃的
plumbing *n.* （建筑物的）管路系统；自来水管道

rip out 扯掉；拔出
scrap *n.* 废料

were out. But they weren't. Two men—Paul Brotherton and Jerry Lucey—were missing.

Just then, McNamee received an *urgent* radio message. It came from Brotherton. He and Lucey were still inside the warehouse. "Mayday! Mayday!" cried Brotherton. "We're running out of air."

McNamee asked where they were. Brotherton said they were on the third floor. There was no way the Worcester crew would just leave them there to die. The other firefighters had to try to rescue them. So McNamee quickly put together several two-person search teams. These teams *headed into* the building to find Brotherton and Lucey. By this time the smoke was so thick the teams had to use *guide ropes* to find their way back outside again.

"We kept *sweeping* and sweeping and sweeping and we still

出来——保罗·布拉特顿和杰瑞·卢塞——失踪了。

　　就在此时，麦克纳米收到了紧急的无线电信号，是布拉特顿发来的，他和卢塞仍然在仓储大楼里面。布拉特顿在无线电里喊道："救命！救命！我们快被呛死了。"

　　麦克纳米问他们两人现在的位置，得到的回答是他们在三楼。伍斯特的消防队员决不会眼睁睁看着自己的队友就这样死去，剩下的人必须尽力去营救这两个人。

　　因此麦克纳米迅速组织了数个小组，每组两名队员。这些小组冲进了大楼去寻找布拉特顿和卢塞。这个时候大楼里面的烟已经十分浓厚，他们不得不用导向绳以便能找到再次出来的路。

　　"我们一直寻找、寻找再寻找，还是没有发现他们两个人。"麦克

---

urgent *adj.* 紧急的　　　　　　　　　head into 走向
guide rope 导向绳　　　　　　　　　　sweep *v.* 彻底搜查

couldn't find them," recalled McNamee. "It's like being in a maze. Zero *visibility*. High heat. Fire. That's what [the search teams] were facing." At last, McNamee told the teams to get out. He didn't want to lose any more people.

But the *nightmare* was getting worse. Four men from the search teams couldn't make it out of the building. They were Timothy Jackson, James Lyons, Joseph McGuirk, and Thomas Spencer. So now a total of six men were trapped inside the flaming warehouse. A *sickening* feeling settled over the other firefighters. They knew their *comrades* were dying inside the building. But there was nothing more they could do.

News of the fire had spread quickly. Hundreds of firefighters from nearby towns arrived on the scene. But they, too, were helpless to

---

纳米队长事后回忆当时的情景说，"就像在迷宫里面一样，能见度为零。酷热，大火，这就是（搜救队）所面对的。"最后麦克纳米告诉队员们退出来，他不想再有任何伤亡了。

可是梦魇越来越让人恐惧了，四名搜救队的队员没能从大楼里撤出来，他们是蒂莫西·杰克逊、詹姆斯·里昂、约瑟夫·麦克古尔克和托马斯·斯班塞。现在一共有六个人被困在火舌笼罩的仓储大楼里面，一种不祥的感觉涌上了外面消防队员的心头。他们知道自己的伙伴可能永远也出不来了，而他们却无能为力。

火灾的消息迅速传开，附近城镇的数百名消防队员纷纷赶到了现场，

---

visibility　*n.* 能见度
sickening　*adj.* 令人厌恶的

nightmare　*n.* 噩梦；梦魇
comrade　*n.* 同志

save the six men. Firefighters kept *dousing* the warehouse with water. But the fire had eaten through the entire building. Soon all the floors collapsed onto each other.

All night the fire raged. The next morning, smoke and flames were still leaping into the air. At last, in the middle of the day, the flames finally began to die down. Only then could firefighters get inside the ruined building. They were able to *recover* the body of Timothy Jackson. But the wreckage of the building was so great that it took a week to find all the other bodies.

The *tragic* death of the six firefighters *stunned* the city of Worcester. The day after the men died, Mayor Raymond Mariano said, "This morning the sun didn't rise. It didn't rise because last night we lost six members of our family."

但是他们也束手无策。队员们不停地用水浇这座仓储大楼，但是火焰已经完全吞没了它，很快，所有的地板都倒塌下去堆成一堆。

大火肆虐了整整一夜。第二天早晨，烟火仍然向空中蹿出。一直到中午，火势才逐渐停止。这时候，消防队员们才得以进入这座毁灭了的建筑物。他们只发现了蒂莫西·杰克逊的尸体，因为大楼坍塌的废墟太庞大了，直到一周以后，其他队员的尸体才被全部找到。

六名救火队员死亡的悲剧震惊了整个伍斯特城。队员们牺牲的第二天，市长雷蒙德·马利亚诺说："今天早晨太阳没有升起来。太阳没有升起来是因为昨天晚上我们这个家庭失去了六名成员。"

---

douse *v.* 泼（或洒、浇）液体在……上

tragic *adj.* 悲剧的

recover *v.* 找回

stun *v.* 使震惊

The fallen men left behind five widows and 17 children. *Sympathy* and money poured in for them. People were especially touched to learn about *The Fireman's Prayer*. This *prayer* hung in the home that Paul Brotherton had shared with his wife and six sons.

The prayer read, "When I am called to duty, God, wherever flames may rage, give me strength to save some life. And if according to your will I have to lose my life, please *bless* with your protecting hand my children and my wife."

Mourning for the dead men spread beyond the city of Worcester. The rest of the nation also felt the loss. It was the highest U.S. firefighter death toll in a burning building in more than 20 years. In fact, firefighters around the world *grieved* for the fallen men. More than 30,000 came to Worcester to honor them. Firefighters came

---

　　牺牲的队员身后留下了五个寡妇和十七个孩子。慰问和捐款像雪片一样从四面八方向他们飞来。当人们看到那篇名为消防员的祈祷的留言的时候，更是无比动容。这篇祈祷的文章就挂在消防员保罗·布拉特顿的家里，他和他的妻子以及六个儿子都能够看到。

　　祈祷这样写道："当我要去履行我的职责的时候，我的上帝，无论火魔在哪里发威，请赐予我力量吧，我要拯救更多的生命。如果按照您的旨意我必须死去的话，那么请用您那无所不能的手保护我的妻子和孩子永远平安。"

　　很快，悲恸之情传出了伍斯特城，举国上下都为六名牺牲的消防员哀悼。这是20年来美国消防官兵在扑灭建筑大火中伤亡最为惨重的一次。事

---

sympathy　*n.* 同情；慰问

bless　*v.* 保佑

prayer　*n.* 祈祷文

grieve　*v.* 使悲伤；感到痛苦

from as far away as Ireland and Australia. As one New Jersey firefighter said, "We came to show we care."

The six Worcester firefighters were true heroes. Mayor Mariano put it this way: "Heroes are not *individuals* who bounce basketballs or hit baseballs in front of thousands of screaming *fans*... . Heroes are average men and women who *reach out unselfishly* to help those in need."

实上，全世界的消防官兵都为这六名葬身火海的队员悲伤。超过三万名队员更是亲自来到伍斯特向他们表达敬意。这些同行最远的来自爱尔兰和澳大利亚，就像一位来自新泽西的消防员说的："我们来就是要表明我们很在意。"

　　六名伍斯特的消防队员是真正的英雄。马里亚诺市长是这样表达的："英雄不是那些在数以千计尖叫的球迷面前耍弄篮球或者击打棒球的人；而是那些在别人需要的时候无私伸出援助双手的普通男人或者女人。"

---

individual *n.* 个人；个体
reach out 伸出

fan *n.* 粉丝；迷
unselfishly *adv.* 无私地

16

Terror at the YMCA

David Bortolotto thought he heard a loud crack. He looked up at the *ceiling*, but it looked fine. So he went back to work.

Bortolotto was a *lifeguard* at the *YMCA* pool in West Roxbury, Massachusetts. At 2 P.M. on September 18, 1989, he was in

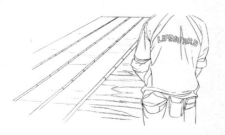

Rescue workers at the scene at the West Roxbury, Massachusetts, YMCA shortly after the ceiling collapsed.

祸从天降

马萨诸塞州西罗克斯贝里的基督教青年会发生顶棚坍塌事故，救援人员旋即赶到现场。

大卫·鲍特洛特感觉听到了一阵巨大的爆裂声音。他抬头看了看天花板，但是没有觉察到什么异样，所以又回去工作了。

鲍特洛特是马萨诸塞州西罗克斯贝里基督教青年会游泳池的救生员。当时是1989年9月18日下午两点，他正在55英尺长的游泳池浅水区教九名

---

ceiling *n.* 天花板　　　　　　　　　　　　　lifeguard *n.* 救生员
YMCA *abbr.* 基督教青年会

the shallow end of the 55-foot swimming *pool*. He was teaching nine young children how to swim. These children ranged in age from 3 to 6.

Some of the children's parents were watching from the *waiting room*. They could see the pool through a glass window. Ellenmarie Joyce could see them too. Joyce was the director of swim classes. She was in her office near the pool.

Suddenly, Bortolotto heard a second loud crack. This time when he looked up, he saw a piece of *concrete* falling from the ceiling. It was headed straight at him and the kids. Quickly, the 18-year-old Bortolotto grabbed a child who was standing on the pool deck just in front of him. He pulled the child toward him into the water. As he did, he *shielded* the child with his own body.

儿童游泳。这些孩子的年龄从三岁到六岁不等。

一些家长在等候室里面等待着他们孩子的训练完毕。他们可以透过一扇玻璃窗户看到里面的训练情形。艾伦玛丽·乔伊斯也能够看到里面的孩子。乔伊斯是游泳培训课堂的主管，她正在游泳池旁边的办公室里。

突然，鲍特洛特又听见了爆裂的声音。这次他一抬头，看见一块混凝土正从天花板上掉下来。他和孩子都听到了声音，这名18岁的救生员立刻抓住了站在他面前池边的一名小男孩，把他拉到身边跳入了水中。此刻，他用自己的身体保护住了小男孩。

---

pool *n.* 水池

concrete *n.* 凝结物

waiting room 等候室

shield *v.* 起保护作用

A piece of the *roof* hit Bortolotto on the head. It opened up a 12-inch gash in his head and took off a chunk of his skin. Blood started to pour out. Yet Bortolotto *barely* noticed this. His heart was racing too fast to feel the pain. His only concern was for the kids in the water. More of the roof was now falling. Concrete, tar, and roofing came rumbling down. Bortolotto swam through the *debris* to guide four children out of the pool. A huge 20-by-15 foot hole had opened up in the roof. Anyone looking up could see the sky.

Joyce, also a trained lifeguard, didn't see the roof collapse. But she heard enough to know there was trouble in the pool. First, she heard the loud bang. Then the laughter and giggles of the children turned into shrill cries of horror. Joyce rushed out of her office to see what was wrong.

一块脱落的屋顶落到了鲍特洛特的头上，划出了一条12英寸长的伤口并且割掉了一大块皮肤，顿时血流如注。而鲍特洛特几乎没有注意到受伤，他的心脏跳动急剧加快以至于都感觉不到伤痛。此时他唯一关注的就是泳池里面的孩子。越来越多的屋顶开始往下落，混凝土、柏油夹杂在屋顶里纷纷向水池中砸来。鲍特洛特拨开落在水中的杂物，带领着四个孩子离开游泳池。这个时候的天花板上出现了一个长20英尺，宽15英尺的大洞，人们一抬头就可以看到外面的天空。

乔伊斯也是一名训练有素的救生员。她没有看到屋顶的塌陷但是听到了巨大的声响，所以她知道游泳池那里一定出问题了。开始的时候乔伊斯听到了"砰"的一声，然后孩子们欢快的笑声就变成了惊恐的尖叫和哭喊，她立刻冲出办公室去看出了什么事。

---

roof *n.* 屋顶   barely *adv.* 几乎不

debris *n.* 碎片

"I just saw David," said Joyce, who had *hired* Bortolotto only two weeks before. "I saw a foot and I saw him looking around, and I just went in." As she dove into the water, Joyce wasn't thinking about her own safety. She was *focused* only on saving the children. "The three closest to me I just grabbed," she said.

Joyce didn't know how many children were in the class. She wasn't sure they were all safe. So she kept diving under the water to look for more.

Some of the parents in the waiting room saw the ceiling give way. One said she saw what looked like bits of *confetti* falling. But it wasn't confetti. What she saw were really bits of ceiling tiles. A second or two later, the roof *caved in*. The parents ran to the door that led to the pool deck. But the door was locked from the outside. They had to

---

在此之前，乔伊斯刚刚雇用了鲍特洛特两周时间。"我只看见了大卫，"乔伊斯事后回忆说，"我看见他的一只脚在水面上，而人正在水下搜寻孩子，随即我也跳了下去。"当她潜入到水下的时候，根本没有考虑到个人的安危，只是想着去救孩子。她说："我正好抓住了离我最近的三个孩子。"

乔伊斯不知道上课的孩子有多少，她也不确定孩子们是不是都已经安全，所以她一直在水下搜寻其他的孩子。

当时在等候室的一些家长看到了天花板的脱落。一名家长说好像是一团庆典上的五彩纸屑飘落下来。但是那不是纸屑，她所看到的是落下来的砖瓦碎片。一两秒钟以后，房顶塌陷下来。家长们向通往泳池的门口跑去，但是门在外面被锁上了。他们不得不穿过衣帽间赶到了水池边。

---

hire *v.* 雇用　　　　　　　　　　　　　　focus *v.* 注视
confetti *n.* 五彩纸屑　　　　　　　　　　cave in 塌落

run through the locker room to reach the pool.

William Scafani, director of the West Roxbury YMCA, was also in the water at the time. When the ceiling collapsed, he, too, thought of the children. Scafani motioned to a man named William McDonald, who happened to be at the *edge* of the pool. McDonald had come to the pool for a swim. Instead, Scafani was asking him to help look for *injured* children.

Scafani and McDonald quickly swam to the shallow end. By then, a lot of debris had fallen into the water. The men couldn't tell if a child was trapped *underneath* the debris. So again and again they dove under to look.

"It was total *bedlam*," said McDonald later. "Kids were crying and parents [were] screaming. I thought, 'My God, [children] must be

---

西罗克斯贝里基督教青年会的会长威廉·斯卡法尼此时也在水中。当天花板塌陷的时候，他也想到了孩子。当时他看到了一个叫威廉·麦克唐纳的男子碰巧也在泳池边上，麦克唐纳是来这里游泳的。于是，斯卡法尼请他帮助寻找受伤的孩子。

斯卡法尼和麦克唐纳迅速游到了浅水区。那个时候，水上已经落了许多碎片。他们两个无法辨认出碎片下面的水中是否还有孩子困在里面，于是他们就一次一次地潜到水下去寻找。

"游泳池里一片混乱，"麦克唐纳事后说，"孩子哭，大人叫。我当时想，'上帝呀，（孩子们）一定是被困在瓦砾下面了。'所以我跳到水里去寻

---

edge *n.* 边缘　　　　　　　　　　injured *adj.* 受伤的；受损害的
underneath *prep.* 在……下面　　　bedlam *n.* 混乱

trapped [under the debris].' So I jumped in and looked for bodies. We just kept searching until we were sure they were all out."

Bortolotto knew the size of his class. So he did a quick head count. That *proved* that all the children were out of the pool. Two of the kids, it seems, had gotten out on their own.

It was a good thing the adults acted so fast. A few moments after everyone was out of the pool, a second *section* of the roof came crashing down. Luckily, no one was hurt by this *incident*.

Still, enough harm had been done by the first collapse. Seven of the children had been hit by falling debris. Two of them were badly injured. They had fractured *skulls*.

The good news was that no one died. But Bortolotto had come very close. The piece of concrete that hit him nearly killed him. He

---

找他们。一直到确定所有的孩子都已经离开了泳池我们才停止搜寻。"

鲍特洛特知道他们训练班孩子的人数，所以他迅速地清点了一遍人数。事实上所有的孩子都已经出来了。其中有两个孩子好像已经自己离开了。

好在大人们的行动采取得非常迅速。就在所有的人离开游泳池以后不久，又有一块房顶砸了下来。幸运的是这一次没有人受到伤害。

然而，房顶第一次坍塌造成的后果也很严重。七个孩子被跌落的碎片砸伤。其中两名儿童伤势严重，确诊为脑骨断裂。

好消息是最后没有人员死亡。但是鲍特洛特距离死亡很近了，那块砸在头上的混凝土险些要了他的命。伤口一共缝合了100针，如果混凝土再

---

prove *v.* 证明　　　　　　　　　　section *n.* 部分
incident *n.* 事件　　　　　　　　skull *n.* 头盖骨；脑壳

needed 100 *stitches* to close the gash. If the concrete had fallen one inch farther to the right, it would have struck him in the middle of his head.

At first, Bortolotto had no idea how badly hurt he was. When he was under the water looking for kids, he knew he had gotten hit. It was only after everyone was safely out of the pool that Joyce saw his bleeding head. She said, "You look hurt."

"My head sort of hurts," Bortolotto said. He was then placed on a *stretcher* and rushed to the hospital.

Everyone agreed that Bortolotto and Joyce *deserved* a lot of *credit*. Both had risked their lives to make sure no child died. "This could have been much, much worse," said Gerard McHale of the Boston Police. "We owe thanks to a young man and woman who were real American heroes."

往右挪一英寸的话，就正中他的头中间了。

开始鲍特洛特没有意识到他的伤有多严重。当在水下搜寻孩子的时候他知道自己受伤了。直到人们都安全离开游泳池以后乔伊斯才看到鲍特洛特流血的头部，对他说："你好像受伤了。"

"我的头受了点伤。"鲍特洛特回答道。然后他就被放上了担架送到了医院。

所有人都认为鲍特洛特和乔伊斯值得称赞。他们都冒着失去生命的危险来保护孩子不受伤害。"（如果当时采取行动不及时）事故的结果可能会非常非常严重，"波士顿警察局的杰拉德·麦克海尔说，"我们应该向这两个人表示感激，他们才是美国真正的英雄。"

---

stitch *n.* 缝线
deserve *v.* 应得；该得

stretcher *n.* 担架
credit *n.* 赞扬

126

17

Desert Disaster

The local people cried when they heard Sven Hedin's plans. They couldn't believe he was going off into the Mankiller Desert. The desert's real name was Takla Makan, but most people in western China just called it the Mankiller. They said that *evil spirits lurked* in this *vast* stretch of sand. They

The bleak landscape of the Takla Makan desert is similar to that of the Sahara Desert, shown here. Explorer Sven Hedin barely survived a trek across the Takla Makan in 1895.

沙漠中的灾难

塔克拉玛干沙漠冷峻的风光与撒哈拉沙漠很相近，从这里我们就可以看出来。1895年探险家司文·和丁从塔克拉玛干沙漠中幸存。

当人们听说司文·和丁的计划时，都哭了起来。他们无法相信他要穿越吃人的大沙漠。这个沙漠的真名叫做塔克拉玛干沙漠，但是住在中国西部的人们干脆叫它"吃人的大沙漠"。他们说，这片沙漠中有妖魔鬼怪在四处游荡。它们使旅行者误入歧途，然后让他们自己死去。

evil spirit 恶魔　　　　　　　　　　　　lurk v. 潜行；鬼鬼祟祟地走
vast adj. 广阔的

said that the spirits led travelers *astray* and then left them to die.

Hedin did not believe the stories. Still, the Swedish explorer felt a strong pull to *investigate* this Asian desert. As he wrote, "I had fallen under the spell of the *weird* witchcraft of the desert." For him, the biggest thrill would be walking where no human had ever walked before. "I knew that beyond the sand dunes, amid the grave-like silence, stretched the unknown, *enchanted* land ..." It was "land that I was going to be the first to tread."

And so, in April of 1895, Hedin set out. With him went a servant named Islam Bai. This man had traveled with Hedin on several previous expeditions. Three local men had also agreed to go. One was a scout named Yollchi. He had been into the desert before in

---

　　和丁不相信这个传言。这位瑞典探险家感到一股强烈的兴趣在吸引着他去探索这个亚洲的大沙漠。就如同他所写的：“我已经被沙漠的神奇巫术所特有的咒语所迷住了。”对他来说，最大的刺激就是在没有人曾经走过的地方探索。“我知道，在沙丘的后面，在墓地一般的寂静中，延伸着不为人知的，神秘的土地……”“我将是第一个踏上那片土地的人。”

　　这样在1895年4月，和丁出发了。他带了一个随从伊兰·白，这个人曾经与和丁在以前的探险活动中共同旅行过。三个当地人同意一同前往，其中一个男孩叫作尤奇，他以前到沙漠里淘过金。他声称可以毫无问题地

---

astray *adv.* 误入歧途地
weird *adj.* 怪异的

investigate *v.* 调查；研究
enchanted *adj.* 施过魔法的

search of gold. He claimed that he could get Hedin across it with no trouble. The group took eight strong *camels*, each packed with water casks, food, and other supplies.

At first, the journey went well. On the third day the group came across a spring. Happily they refilled their water casks. By the sixth day they had gone more than 50 miles. "We were getting farther and farther into the unknown ocean of *sandy* desert," wrote Hedin. "Not a sign of life to be seen, not a sound to be heard ..."

On the tenth day, April 20, the group came to an *oasis*. Here they found pools of water and thick green *grass*. Yollchi told Hedin that they were near the Khotan River. He said that they should reach it within four days. Once they got there, they would have all the water they needed for the rest of the trip.

把和丁带出沙漠。这个探险队带了八头强壮的骆驼，每一头骆驼上驮了水桶、食品和其他的用品。

刚开始，旅程还算顺利。在第三天，他们经过了一条小河。他们十分高兴地给水桶装满水。到了第六天，他们已经走出了50英里。"在这片沙海中我们越走越远，"和丁写道，"没有任何生命的迹象，没有任何声音……"

在第十天，也就是4月20日，他们来到了一片绿洲。他们在这里找到了池塘和厚实的草地。尤奇告诉和丁，他们已经接近了考滩河。他说他们再有四天就能到达，只要一到那里，他们就能够得到他们剩会旅程所需要的所有淡水。

---

camel *n.* 骆驼

oasis *n.* 绿洲

sandy *adj.* 沙地的

grass *n.* 草；草地

Hedin was thrilled. It seemed that they would make it to the eastern end of the desert without difficulty. He even decided to give the camels a break. He ordered the water *casks* filled just halfway to the top. That would *ease* the *burden* on the tired animals, and it would still be more than enough for the group. Hedin figured half-full casks would last them 10 days.

Unfortunately, Yollchi was wrong. The Khotan River was not four days away. It was a full 15 days' journey from where the men stood. On April 24 Hedin and his men ran into a terrible *sandstorm*. "Clouds and columns of sand whirled in a mad dance across the desert," he wrote. "The fine red drift-sand penetrated everywhere—into mouth, nose, ears ..."

The next day Hedin discovered that they were almost out of

和丁感到十分兴奋，看起来，他们可以毫无困难地到达沙漠的东端。他甚至决定让骆驼休息一下。他命令水只装半桶，这样可以让疲惫的牲畜得以休息，同时又足够全队人员的饮用。和丁计算半桶的水可以坚持10天。

不幸的是，尤奇犯了个错误。考滩河不在4天的路程之内，从他们的所在地，他们要走整整15天。从4月24日开始，和丁和他的人进入到了一片可怕的沙暴中。"沙土的风暴把沙漠吹得天昏地暗，"他写道，"红色的浮尘钻入了任何的缝隙——嘴、鼻子、耳朵……"

第二天，和丁发现他们几乎没有水了。原来仆人们没有把水桶添到一

---

cask *n.* 桶
burden *n.* 负担

ease *v.* 减轻；缓和
sandstorm *n.* 沙暴

water. It turned out that the servants hadn't filled the water casks all the way to the halfway mark. Grimly, Hedin cut everyone's water *rations* way down. The group dug deep into the sand, looking for a well or a spring, but they found nothing. Knowing they couldn't properly water eight thirsty camels, they decided to leave two behind. Then they hurried on through the hot, *dusty* desert, hoping to reach the Khotan River soon.

By April 30 they were in real trouble. It had been 10 days since they left had the oasis. They were now totally out of water. They had also *dumped* most of their food to lighten their load. "We are all terribly weak, men as well as camels," wrote Hedin in his diary that day. "God help us all!"

The next day brought another *endless* walk through the scorching

---

半的位置。和丁严肃地把每个人的饮用水配额削减到最低。探险队向下掘水，寻找泉眼，但是什么也没有发现。他们知道无法给八头口渴的骆驼提供足够的饮用水，决定放掉两头。然后他们匆忙地走入炎热、布满浮尘的大漠之中，希望能够早日找到考滩河。

到了4月30日，他们遇到了真正的难题。他们已经离开绿洲十天了，现在完全断水了。他们也把大部分食品抛掉了来轻装。"我们都极度虚弱，骆驼也是，"那一天和丁在日记中记载道，"上帝救救我们吧！"

第二天，他们在酷热的大漠中又艰难地行进了一天。和丁一直在扫视

---

ration *n.* 定量
dump *v.* 扔掉

dusty *adj.* 落满灰尘的
endless *adj.* 无止境的

heat. Hedin kept scanning the *horizon*, but he saw no sign of the Khotan River. One of the men became *convinced* that evil spirits had led them in the wrong direction. All of them were growing nervous. They were no longer sure they would get out of this desert alive.

Later that day they couldn't stand their thirst any longer. They decided to drink some strong Chinese *brandy*, which they had been using to fuel their stove. The strong drink made them all sick. It even killed one of the men.

By May 3 most of the camels were dead, and Yollchi had disappeared. Somewhere on the long, hot march he had fallen behind and now he had completely dropped out of sight. Neither Hedin nor the others had the *strength* to turn back for him. That same day, Islam Bai collapsed. He was too weak to walk. Hedin

---

着地平线，但是他没有看到水的迹象。他们其中的一个人开始相信一定是什么妖魔鬼怪使他们误入歧途。他们的神经开始紧张起来，不再确信他们能活着走出沙漠了。

这天的下午，他们再也无法忍受口渴的煎熬，决定喝一些度数很高的中国白酒。在旅程中他们用白酒做炉子的燃料，白酒的酒精使他们不正常起来。他们甚至杀死了一个人。

到5月3日，大部分的骆驼都死了，尤奇也消失了。在长途行进中，他掉队了，现在已经完全消失。和丁和其他的人都没有力气去回头救他。就在那一天，伊兰·白也倒下了。他太虚弱，已经不能走了。和丁非常伤

---

horizon *n.* 地平线　　　　　　　　convinced *adj.* 坚定不移的；确信的
brandy *n.* 白兰地（酒）　　　　　　strength *n.* 力量

was heartbroken, but he had no choice. He left Islam Bai with the last camel and a few provisions. Then he and his remaining servant, Kasim, stumbled on alone.

Finally, on May 5, Hedin *glimpsed* trees in the distance. That meant there was water up ahead. Leaving Kasim to rest, Hedin dragged himself through the blazing sun toward the trees. When he reached them, he sank down *next to* the Khotan River. He drank and drank until he could drink no more. Then he took off his *boots* and filled them with water. Carefully he carried them back to Kasim so he, too, could have a drink.

For Hedin, the worst was over. Now that he had water, his strength returned. The next day he and Kasim met some *shepherds* who gave them food and shelter. Four days after that he and Kasim

---

心，但是他别无选择。他给伊兰·白留下了最后一头骆驼和一些供给。然后他和他的最后一名仆人，卡希姆，蹒跚着又上路了。

最后，在5月5日，和丁看到了远方的树林，说明那里有水。他留下卡希姆休息，和丁坚持在烈日下向树林前进。他到达树林后，就倒在了考滩河边。他喝啊喝啊，直到再也喝不下去了为止。然后他脱下靴子，装满水，小心地把它送到卡希姆那里，这样，他也能喝上水。

对于和丁来说，最糟糕的时候已经过去。因为他有水，他的力量又恢复了。第二天，他和卡希姆遇到了一些牧羊人，牧羊人为他们提供了食物和住处。接下来的四天，他和卡希姆一直在考滩河河岸上休息。他们看到

---

glimpse *v.* 瞥见；看一眼
boot *n.* 靴子

next to 紧挨着
shepherd *n.* 牧羊人

were resting by the bank of the Khotan River. In the distance he saw another group of shepherds walking toward them. To Hedin's joy, these shepherds had Islam Bai with them!

When Islam Bai reached Hedin, he explained that the shepherds had found him as he lay in the sand. They had given him food and water. They had also *rescued* his camel. In the camel's bags were Hedin's diary and maps, so the record of the group's journey was saved.

A few days later Sven Hedin, Islam Bai, and Kasim at last walked out of the desert. They had done what they set out to do. They had crossed Takla Makan, the Mankiller desert. But two people and seven camels had died along the way. And even for those who survived, it had been a very *grim* journey indeed.

远方有另外一群牧羊人向他们走来。令和丁大喜过望的是，伊兰·白和他们在一起！

伊兰·白向和丁解释道，那些牧羊人在沙漠中找到了他。他们给他水和食物。他们也把他的骆驼救活了。在骆驼的驮袋中有和丁的日记和地图，这样他们团队的记录被保留了下来。

几天以后，司文·和丁、伊兰·白和卡希姆终于走出了沙漠。他们终于实现了目标，通过了塔克拉玛干大沙漠，这是名副其实的"吃人的沙漠"。其中，两个人，七匹骆驼死在了路上。而且对于他们这些幸存下来的人来说，这也的确是个艰苦的旅程。

---

rescue *v.* 营救　　　　　　　　　　　　　　　　grim *adj.* 残酷的

18

Trapped in the Himalayas

Pilots called it the "*hump*." That was an innocent-sounding name, but the reality was *fearful*. During World War II some pilots said they would rather fight Japanese war planes than challenge the hump. The "hump" was the *Himalayan Mountains*. Pilots had to fly over these Asian

The majestic peaks of the Himalayan Mountains offer little shelter to people stranded on them. Amazingly, Captains Rosbert and Hammel survived for several weeks in these mountains after their plane crashed into a mountain peak.

被困喜马拉雅

巍峨的喜马拉雅山脉中的山峰几乎没有给那里的人们提供一点居住地。令人惊奇的是罗思波特和哈米尔上尉的飞机在山中坠毁后竟然幸存了几个星期并最终获救。

飞行员把它叫作"驼峰"。听起来这个名字没有什么，但是现实是恐怖的。在第二次世界大战期间，一些飞行员说他们宁愿与日本飞行员交战也不愿意挑战这些"驼峰"。"驼峰"就是喜马拉雅山脉的群山。飞行员要飞过这些亚洲的高山——这是世界上最高的山脉——去给中国盟国送去

hump *n.* 驼峰
Himalayan Mountain 喜马拉雅山脉

fearful *adj.* 可怕的

mountains—the highest in the world—to bring food and supplies to their Chinese *allies*.

How dangerous was the hump? In the early 1940s, 850 people died trying to fly over these mountains. The single worst day came in 1944 when nine planes crashed. The planes were not *shot down*. They simply crashed into the mountains. Planes in those days were not *as good as* they are today. The Douglas C-47s had to strain to get high enough to clear the peaks. Some pilots joked *grimly* that they could plot their course by the line of smoking wrecks.

On April 7, 1943, Captain C.Joseph Rosbert took off in thick fog from India to fly over the "hump." His co-pilot was Captain Charles "Ridge" Hammel. A Chinese radio operator named Li Wong was also on board. As the plane neared the peak, Hammel reached back and

---

食品和用品。

　　驼峰有多么危险？在20世纪40年代，有850人在尝试飞越此航线时遇难。最糟糕的一天发生在1944年，当天九架飞机坠毁。这些飞机不是被击落的，而是撞在了山峰上。那时的飞机并没有今天的好，道格拉斯C-47飞机想要飞越顶峰很费劲。一些飞行员开玩笑说，他们可以看着冒烟的飞机残骸作为路标来前进。

　　1943年4月7日，C·约瑟夫·罗思波特上尉在印度的浓雾中起飞，来飞越"驼峰"航线。他的副驾驶是查尔斯·里奇·哈米尔上尉，一名中国无线电话务员李宏也在飞机上。当飞机接近顶峰时，哈米尔向后靠了

---

ally *n.* 同盟国

as good as 一样好

shoot down 击落；打垮

grimly *adv.* 严肃地

gave Wong a reassuring pat. "We're O.K. now," he said. "Another thousand feet and we'll be clear of the hump. Another hour and you'll be home."

But they never made that thousand feet. Clouds moved in, and ice formed on the *windshield*. Ice also built up on the wings. Soon six *inches* of ice were weighing the plane down. The plane started to drop slowly. Rosbert pressed one hand to the windshield, hoping to melt the ice. He cleared a peephole two inches wide. Suddenly the cloud lifted, and Rosbert saw a jagged peak straight ahead. "Look out!" he yelled. "There's a mountain."

Rosbert banked the plane sharply as he kept his eyes on the tiny *peephole*. The plane missed hitting the peak by inches. But it *swerved* right toward a neighboring mountain. There was a terrible scraping

---

靠，轻轻拍了一下李宏，"我们现在没有问题，"他说，"再升高1000英尺，我们就超过这些驼峰了。再过一个小时，你就到家了。"

但是他们再也没有升高1000英尺。云朵在附近聚集，挡风玻璃上开始结冰。机翼上也开始结冰。很快飞机上结了6英寸的冰层，把飞机坠了下来。飞机开始慢慢下降。罗思波特把手按在挡风玻璃上希望能融化冰层。他融化出了一个两英尺宽的窥视孔。突然云层移开了，罗思波特看到一座锯齿状的山峰就出现在前面。"小心！"他大喊着，"前面有山。"

罗思波特眼睛紧紧盯住小窥视孔，驾驶飞机急速转弯。飞机几乎是就差几英寸的距离就撞到了山上，但是它转了过来直接朝另一座山峰撞去。一阵剧烈的刮擦声传来，机组人员感觉他们自己向前冲去。引擎发出了狂暴的

---

windshield *n.* 挡风玻璃　　　　　　　inch *n.* 英寸
peephole *n.* 窥视孔　　　　　　　　　swerve *v.* 转弯

noise. The men felt themselves thrown forward. The engines raced with a *violent roar*. Then, just as suddenly, everything fell quiet.

It took Hammel and Rosbert a couple of seconds to realize that they were still alive.

"What happened?" asked Hammel.

"We hit a mountain," answered Rosbert. Indeed, the plane had crashed sideways along the face of a cliff. Rosbert was surprised that they had survived; by all rights, he thought, they should be dead.

Sadly, the crash did end the life of Li Wong. The *collision* had broken his neck. Meanwhile, Hammel's face and hands were dripping blood. His left *ankle* was badly sprained. Rosbert, too, had

---

轰鸣声。然后突然之间，一切都陷入寂静。

　　哈米尔和罗思波特过了几分钟才意识到他们还活着。

　　"怎么回事？"哈米尔说。

　　"我们撞到了一座山峰，"罗思波特说。的确，飞机斜刮到了一个山崖的侧面。罗思波特非常奇怪的是他们还活着；他本来想，他们死定了。

　　可悲的是，撞击的确夺走了李宏的生命。撞击折断了他的脖子。当时，哈米尔的脸上和手上都在滴血，他左脚的脚踝部受到了严重的扭伤，至少有一块骨头折断了。如果说他们能在这次撞击事件中幸存下来，这是

---

violent *adj.* 猛烈的
collision *n.* 撞击

roar *n.* 咆哮；吼叫
ankle *n.* 踝关节

hurt his left ankle. At least one *bone* had snapped. If it was a miracle that they had survived the crash, it would take a second miracle for them to *get off* this 16,000-foot mountain.

Rosbert and Hammel talked about what to do. They thought their chances of being seen and rescued were slim. They had no warm clothing and only enough food for a few days. When the sky cleared, they could see the tree line below. It was about 5,000 feet down and *at least* five miles away. If they could get there, they might find a *stream*. Then they could follow the stream down and maybe find a village. They decided that as soon as they could, they would head down toward those trees.

At the moment, though, neither man could walk. Their ankles hurt too much. So they stayed in the shelter of the plane. They

---

第一个奇迹，那么他们能从这个16,000英尺高的山上下来，就是第二个奇迹。

　　罗思波特和哈米尔商量了一下该如何进行下一步。他们想，能够被看到，得到营救的机会实在是太小了。他们没有保暖的衣物，只有几天的食物。当天空放晴时，他们能够看到下面生长着树木的雪线下部。那大约是5000英尺的下面，至少要走5英里。如果他们能够到达那里，可能会找到小溪。然后他们可以沿着小溪前进。可能会找到一个村庄。他们决定尽快朝着那片树林前进。

　　当时，他们俩都不能行走，他们的脚踝伤得太严重了，所以待在飞机

---

bone *n.* 骨头
at least 至少

get off 从……下来
stream *n.* 小溪

figured that in five days their ankles might be *healed* enough to begin walking. By the third day, however, they couldn't stand the wait. They decided to *head down* the *mountainside*.

Each step was agony. After 200 yards they realized that they would never reach the tree line by nightfall. Knowing that they wouldn't survive a night in the open, they turned back. They were lucky to get back to the plane before dark.

The next morning Rosbert and Hammel used bits of wood from the plane to make *splints* for their legs. They hoped that would ease the pain of walking. They also used the wood to fashion a couple of crude sleds. The sleds didn't work very well; they went too fast and were impossible to control. But the men discovered that they could slide on the seat of their pants, going 20 or 30 yards at a time. In this

---

里。他们计算着五天之内脚踝就应该好起来，可以走路了。但是到了第三天，他们不能再等，决定向山下前进。

　　每一步都是极大的痛苦。行进了200码以后，他们意识到在天黑之前不可能到达树木带。而且他们知道不可能在外面活过一个夜晚，所以返了回来，并十分幸运地在天黑之前回到了飞机。

　　第二天早晨，罗思波特和哈米尔使用从飞机上卸下来的小块木头为他们的腿做成夹板。他们希望这样能够减轻行走时的痛苦。他们还用木头做了一对简易的雪橇，雪橇不是很好用；它们滑得太快，无法控制。但是他们发现可以干脆坐在地上，一次滑行前进20—30码，这样他们缓慢地滑

---

heal *v.* 治愈
mountainside *n.* 山坡

head down 朝下；向下
splint *n.* 夹板

way they made their way slowly down the mountain.

As they neared the tree line they reached a very *steep* 500-foot slope. There was no way to get around it. They would have to go straight down and hope for the best. Hammel went first, disappearing in a cloud of snow. All Rosbert heard was a loud scream. Moments later, Hammel shouted out, "It's OK, but it's rough. Come on down."

Hammel took a deep breath, *shoved* off with his good leg, and began sailing down the slope. "Finally, I hit *solid* earth with a crunching jolt," he later said. "As I lay there, afraid my back was broken, I heard the sound of rushing water." The men's spirits rose. They had found a river.

For three days they *hobbled* along, following the river. By now all

---

下了山坡。

　　当他们接近树木带时，接近了一个非常陡峭，大约500英尺长的山坡。没有办法绕行，他们只能直接滑下去，希望上帝保佑。哈米尔第一个走，消失在一片雪雾中。罗思波特只听到一阵高声尖叫。过了一会，哈米尔的喊声又出现了："没事，就是很颠簸，下来吧！"

　　哈米尔做了个深呼吸，用他能用的腿推住，开始向坡下滑行。"最后，我颠簸着冲上了坚硬的土地，"后来他说，"我躺在那里害怕后背骨折，我听到了激流的小河。"他们的意志恢复了起来，发现了一条小河。

　　他们一瘸一拐地沿着小河走了三天，现在所有的食物都吃光了，必须尽

---

steep *adj.* 陡峭的
solid *adj.* 牢固的；结实的

shove *v.* 推；推动
hobble *v.* 一瘸一拐地走路

their food was gone. They had to find help soon or they would die. When the *riverbanks* became too steep, they moved down into the river itself.

Then they came to a series of dangerous *waterfalls*. They couldn't walk in the water any longer, but on both sides of them rose sheer walls of rock. How could they ever get out? Their situation appeared hopeless.

Then Hammel leaned forward. He had *spotted* a *vine* hanging off one of the cliffs. After pulling on it, he and Rosbert decided it might be sturdy enough to hold them. Besides, it was their only chance. "Foot by foot," said Rosbert, "we pulled and clambered our way up the wall." At the top they found an encouraging sign of human life. Someone had notched the trees as though marking a trail.

快寻求到帮助，否则就死定了。当河岸变得太陡峭时，他们就在河里面走。

后来他们来到了一系列危险的瀑布旁边，不能再在河流里面走了，但是他们的身旁耸立着两扇陡峭的峭壁。怎么才能出去呢？情况看起来是令人绝望的。

哈米尔探出身子，向下看，发现一条藤条从一个峭壁上垂了下来。他们拉了拉它，觉得能够承受住。而且那是他们唯一的机会。"一点一点地，"罗思波特说，"我们拉着藤条爬下了峭壁。"在下面他们发现了人的痕迹，得到了极大的鼓舞。有人在树上刻画了凹口，好像是在标示一个路径。

---

riverbank　*n.*　河堤　　　　　　　　　　waterfall　*n.*　瀑布
spot　*v.*　发现　　　　　　　　　　　　vine　*n.*　藤

For the next several days the two men dragged themselves along, still following the river. Thirteen days after the crash, they came to a *fork* in the river. They weren't sure which way to go but at last decided to head east, the same direction they had been traveling all along. It was a lucky choice. Within an hour the men had stumbled upon a hut. It was burned to the ground, but at least it showed that people had once lived here. With renewed strength Hammel and Rosbert kept walking. Just before night they came to another hut. This one, thankfully, had people inside. The people looked like they had stepped out of the *Stone Age*. They had broad, flat *foreheads* and *mops* of long, shaggy hair. They were very hospitable and interested in their visitors. They gave Hammel and Rosbert food and a place to sleep. In return, the men let their hosts feel their clothes and look at

---

接下来几天，两个人相互搀扶着沿着小河向前走。在飞机坠毁的第十三天，他们来到了小河的一个河汊处，不知道该向哪里走，但是最后他们决定向东走，这也是他们一直飞行的方向。这是个很幸运的选择。一个小时后，他们蹒跚地来到一个小屋的前面。它已经被烧毁了，残破地倒在地面上，但是至少说明曾经有人在这里生活过。哈米尔和罗思波特又燃起了希望，继续向前走。就在夜幕降临之前，他们又来到另一个小屋的前面。感谢上帝，这个小屋里面有人。这里的人好像是从石器时代来的，前额宽阔扁平，头发浓密杂乱。他们对来客十分友好，也很感兴趣，给哈米尔和罗思波特食品和睡觉的地方。作为回报，他们让主人们摸了摸他们的

---

fork *n.* 分叉；分支
forehead *n.* 前额

Stone Age 石器时代
mop *n.* 蓬乱的头发

their watches and flashlights.

For the next several days they stayed in the *remote* village. Although the people treated them very well, the men were still eager to get home. The natives helped them *hike* 16 more days to get out of the mountains. Finally, 47 days after the crash, they made it back to their base in India. No one could believe that they had survived such an ordeal. It was, as one magazine put it, "one chance in a million."

衣服，看了看他们的手表和电筒。

　　过去的几天里，他们一直住在这个偏远的小山村里面。虽然这里的人们对他们很好，他们还是渴望能够早日回到家乡。当地人帮助他们走了16天的山路走出了群山。最后在坠毁后的第47天，他们回到了印度的基地。没有人能够相信他们居然在这样的灾难中幸存。这就如同一本杂志中所说的："是百万分之一的机会。"

---

remote *adj.* 偏僻的；遥远的　　　　　　　　　　hike *v.* 远足；徒步旅行

19

All Alone in the Jungle

Juliane Koepcke was *looking forward to* Christmas. The 17-year-old had just finished high school in Lima, Peru. Now she was headed back to her parents' house. She couldn't wait to get there. Mr. and Mrs. Koepcke lived deep in the Peruvian *jungle*. Although the

The rivers of the Peruvian jungle wind through miles of uninhabited land.

独步丛林

秘鲁丛林中的河流在荒无人烟的地带蜿蜒而行。

朱利安·科伊普克盼望着过圣诞节。她今年17岁了，刚刚在利马上完中学。现在她正在返回她父母家的路上，她太盼望回到家里了。科伊普克夫妇生活在秘鲁丛林的深处，他们都是德国人，花了多年的时间在亚马孙河流域研究野生动植物。

---

look forward to 期待

jungle *n.* 丛林

Koepckes were German, they had spent years studying wildlife along the Amazon.

Mrs. Koepcke flew to Lima to help her daughter *pack up*. Then she and Juliane headed to the airport for the 90-minute flight to the jungle town of Pucallpa. It was Christmas Eve, 1971. Juliane had *dressed up* for the occasion. She wore a frilly white dress and her best high-heeled shoes. About *midday* she climbed into a Lockheed Electra plane. Then she took her seat next to the window, three rows from the back. Her mother sat in the seat next to her.

The flight seemed to go smoothly. There was no hint of trouble as the plane *approached* Pucallpa. The passengers were told to put on their seat belts for landing. Then, without warning, the plane flew into a violent jungle storm.

"Suddenly we heard a loud noise," recalled Juliane later. "Looking

---

科伊普克夫人乘飞机到利马帮助女儿打好包裹。然后她和朱利安向机场出发，她们飞90分钟就可以到达丛林中的小城普卡帕。当时是1971年的圣诞节前夜。朱利安已经穿上了迎接节日的服装，镶有褶边的白色服装和她最好的高跟鞋。大约在中午，她们钻进洛克西德·伊莱克特拉飞机。她坐在倒数第三排靠窗子的座椅上，她妈妈坐在她旁边的座位上。

飞机看起来飞行平稳。飞机已经接近了普卡帕，旅客得到通知要求系上安全带，准备降落。突然在毫无警示的情况下，飞机遇到了热带丛林中的风暴。

"突然我们听到一阵剧烈的噪音，"朱利安后来回忆道，"从机窗向

---

pack up 整理；把……打包   dress up 穿上盛装
midday *n.* 中午   approach *v.* 接近

out of the window I saw that the right wing was on fire."

Terrified, Juliane turned to her mother. Mrs. Koepcke looked at her daughter and said, "This is the end of everything." These were the last words Mrs. Koepcke would ever speak.

Juliane later said, "The next thing I knew, it felt like I was sitting in the air and then everything went black."

The plane had exploded in *midair*. Ninety-one of the 92 people on board died in the blast. Only Juliane Koepcke survived. She landed on the jungle floor, still *strapped* to her seat. Her only injuries were a broken *collarbone* and a cut on her upper right arm. Experts say it is almost impossible to survive such a fall. Yet somehow Koepcke did it.

At first Juliane was in a *daze*. She lay in her seat and called out

---

外看去发现飞机的右翼已经起火。"

　　朱利安非常害怕，扑到了妈妈的怀里。科伊普克夫人看着女儿说："这下全完了。"这是科伊普克夫人说的最后一句话。

　　朱利安后来说："我所知道的下一个情况，就是感觉我好像是飘在空气中，然后突然所有的一切都变黑了。"

　　飞机在空中爆炸了。机上92人中91人在爆炸中丧生。只有朱利安·科伊普克幸存了下来。她降落在一片丛林的地面上，安全带一直牢固地把她固定在座椅上。她仅受了点轻伤：锁骨骨折、右胳膊上部划伤。专家们说在这样的降落中能够幸存简直是不可能的。但是，无论怎样，她做到了。

　　刚开始，朱利安感到一阵眩晕。她躺在椅子上呼救，但是没有人回

---

midair *n.* 半空中
collarbone *n.* 锁骨

strap *v.* 用带捆扎；束牢
daze *n.* 眼花缭乱；目眩

for help, but no one answered. All she heard was the screeching of jungle birds. Then she got out of her seat and *looked around*. She couldn't see well because her glasses had come off in the explosion. Still, she *spotted* some Christmas cakes lying on the ground and ate them hungrily. She looked around for her mother, but Juliane saw no sign of Mrs. Koepcke anywhere. In fact, she saw no sign of human life at all.

As darkness fell, it began to rain. Juliane crept under her airplane seat and *huddled* there throughout the night. The next morning she crawled out again. She knew that if she didn't find a way out of the jungle soon she would die, so she began walking. Before long she *stumbled* upon a row of three airplane seats lying face down. Hoping to find other survivors, Koepcke turned the seats over. Strapped to

---

答，听到的只有丛林中震耳的鸟叫声。然后她从座椅上下来，向周围打量起来。她看得不是很清楚，因为她的眼镜在爆炸中不知道飞到哪去了。最终她还是在地上找到了一些圣诞蛋糕，她非常饥饿就大吃起来。她四处寻找她的妈妈，但是朱利安没有找到科伊普克夫人的痕迹。实际上她压根就没有看到一点人存在的痕迹。

夜幕降临，天开始下雨。朱利安爬到了那个飞机座椅下面，在那里蜷缩了一夜。第二天早晨她爬了出来。她知道如果她不能找到走出丛林的路，很快她就可能死亡，所以她开始向外走。不一会，她跌跌撞撞地来到了一排翻过个的飞机座椅前面。科伊普克希望能找到其他幸存者，她把这些座椅翻

---

look around 到处看   spot *v.* 发现
huddle *v.* 使缩成一团   stumble *v.* 蹒跚；东倒西歪地走

the seats were the dead bodies of three teenage girls, their faces covered with flies.

Feeling sick, Juliane *moved on*, struggling through thick bushes. Branches tore at her dress. Her shoes stuck in the *soggy* ground. Before long, she had lost one shoe completely. From time to time, she heard airplanes high overhead. She thought that they were probably looking for survivors from the crash. But they could not see her through the *dense* jungle *foliage*.

That night Juliane curled up under a tree. The next morning she began walking again. By this time her stomach was rumbling with hunger. She saw several things she thought might be edible, including fruit, mushrooms, even frogs. But her parents had warned her that many things found in the jungle were poisonous. She didn't

---

了过来。座椅上系着的是三个女孩子，她们已经死了，脸上都是苍蝇。

朱利安感到很恶心，她又向前走，努力地通过密实的树丛。树枝划坏了她的衣服，鞋也陷入泥泞的地面。没多久她就完全地丢掉了一只鞋。她总能听到头上有飞机一次又一次地飞过。她想，他们可能是在寻找失事的幸存者。但是，在这样浓密的热带丛林中，他们不可能透过树冠看到她。

那天晚上朱利安蜷缩在一棵树的下面。第二天早晨她又出发了，这时她的肚子饿得咕咕直叫。她看到了一些东西，猜想大概可以食用，其中包括水果、蘑菇、甚至青蛙。但是她的父母曾经警告过她，丛林中的许多东西都是有毒的。她不敢尝哪怕是一点点的东西。

---

move on 往前走　　　　　　　　　　　soggy *adj.* 浸水的；湿润的
dense *adj.* 稠密的；浓密的　　　　　　foliage *n.* 植物；叶子

dare take even a small bite of anything.

Over the next three days, Juliane covered many miles. She finally came to a river and began to follow it, thinking it would lead her to *civilization*. From time to time, she climbed into the water and swam along with the current, thinking that would be easier than walking. When she got out of the water, she felt *leeches* clinging to her body. Several times she passed *crocodiles* along the riverbank, but fortunately they didn't seem very interested in her.

Walking was no better. Her bare feet turned black and blue with bruises. The sun burned her back. Thorns cut into her skin, causing painful infections. Jungle flies burrowed into the open wounds and laid eggs. When the eggs *hatched*, Juliane could feel worms wiggling around underneath her skin.

在以后的三天里，朱利安走了很多英里。最后她来到了一条小河边，开始沿着小河走，她觉得小河可以把她带到有人类文明的地方。她一次又一次地顺着水流游泳，认为这样可以比行走更容易。但是当她从水里出来时，感到有水蛭吸在她的身上。有几次她经过了河岸的鳄鱼，幸运的是，好像它们对她并不感兴趣。

走路也好不到哪儿去。她赤裸的双脚由于擦伤和瘀伤已经青紫。阳光灼伤了她的后背。荆棘划坏了她的皮肤，导致感染。丛林的苍蝇拼命地往她的伤口里面钻，并在里面产卵。当这些卵孵出来时，朱利安能感觉到蠕虫在皮肤下面蠕动。

---

civilization *n.* 文明；文化　　　　　　　　leech *n.* 水蛭

crocodile *n.* 鳄鱼　　　　　　　　　　　　hatch *v.* 孵化

On the fourth day Juliane spotted a lean-to near the edge of the river. Too tired to go any farther, she crawled inside it. The shelter didn't contain any food, but she did find some *kerosene*. She splashed some of it onto her cuts and, using a *splinter* of wood, tried to dig the worms out from under her skin.

For five days Koepcke huddled in the lean-to, growing weaker and weaker. At last, nine days after the crash, she heard voices. Looking out toward the river, she spotted three local hunters paddling by in a *canoe*. Struggling to the riverbank, Juliane managed to call out to them. At first the hunters were reluctant to approach her. Her *gaunt* face and bloodshot eyes frightened them. Also, they were not used to seeing girls with white skin and blond hair. They feared she might be some sort of demon.

　　第四天，朱利安发现河边有一个单坡屋顶的小房子。她太累了，已经没有力气再继续前进，爬到房子的里面。房子里面没有任何食物，但是她找到了一些煤油。于是她把煤油浇到伤口上，试图使用一块木片把皮下的蠕虫挖出来。

　　五天过去了，科伊普克蜷缩在小屋子里，越来越虚弱。最后，在飞机失事的第九天，她听到了人的讲话声。她向河上看，发现一些当地的猎人划着独木舟在河里面行进。朱利安奋力爬到河岸，向他们呼喊。最初，猎人们不愿意靠近她。她憔悴的脸色和充满血丝的眼睛使他们很害怕。而且他们也不习惯看到白皮肤、黄头发的女孩。他们很恐惧地认为她是某种魔鬼。

---

kerosene　*n.*　煤油

canoe　*n.*　独木舟

splinter　*n.*　碎片

gaunt　*adj.*　憔悴的

Finally, though, they *paddled* over to the lean-to. Seeing Juliane's weak condition, they did what they could to help. One man offered her food while another poured *gasoline* over her body to draw out the worms under her skin. "I counted 35 worms that came out of my arms alone," Koepcke later said. Ten more came out of other parts of her body.

The men let Juliane rest overnight and then loaded her into their canoe and headed downriver. Seven and a half hours later they made it to a small *outpost*. At last Koepcke was safe. Plans were made to take her to her father. Rescue teams questioned her about the *location* of the downed plane. When searchers did finally find the remains of the plane, they were shocked. It had exploded into hundreds of bits and pieces. As one searcher said, "Only God knows how that girl survived."

尽管这样，最后，他们还是划向了这个小屋子。看到朱利安虚弱的情况，他们尽力来帮助她。一个人喂给她食物，另一个人把汽油浇在她的身上，来驱赶出皮下的蠕虫。"就只在我的胳膊里面我就数出了35只蠕虫，"科伊普克后来说。身体的其他部分又驱出了10只。

人们让朱利安休息了一夜，然后把她装上他们的独木舟，向下游驶去。七个半小时后他们来到了一个偏远的村落里面。最后，科伊普克安全了，她被送到了父亲身边。营救人员向她询问了失事飞机的地点。当搜索人员到达飞机残骸所在地时，他们都惊呆了。飞机已经爆炸成了成百上千个碎片。一名搜索人员说："只有上帝知道那个女孩是怎么幸存下来的。"

---

paddle *v.* 划桨

outpost *n.* 偏远居民点

gasoline *n.* 汽油

location *n.* 位置

20

Buried in Nairobi

Boom! No one knew what the strange sound was. The workers at the Ufundi Cooperative House in Nairobi, Kenya, all heard it, but no one could *identify* the *source*. Had the noise come from nearby *construction* work? Had it come from a gun? Or had it been a *grenade* blast? Looking for an answer, many people

The Ufundi Cooperative House in Nairobi, Kenya, was completely destroyed in a bomb attack meant for the American Embassy building next to it.

内罗毕惨案

在预谋袭击美国大使馆的爆炸中内罗毕的乌凡第合作大厦被完全摧毁。

砰！没有人知道这个奇怪的声音是从哪里传出来的。所有在肯尼亚内罗毕乌凡第合作大厦里面的工作人员都听到了，但是没有人能够说得清是哪里发出的。是附近的建筑工地发出的？还是枪声？还是手榴弹的爆炸声？为了寻找答案，大楼里面许多人冲到了窗前想看个究竟。当时的时间

identify *v.* 确定　　　　　　　　　　source *n.* 来源
construction *n.* 建筑物　　　　　　　grenade *n.* 手榴弹

in the building rushed toward the windows. It was about 10:30 in the morning on Friday, August 7, 1998.

Gaitara Ng'ang'a [pronounced enyah-ENYAH] was as curious as everyone else. The 48-year-old scrap-metal dealer did not work in the Ufundi House. He had just dropped by to see a friend. Still, he was *curious* about the noise he had heard and joined the crowd of people *scurrying* to the windows. Ng'ang'a tried to see out, but he couldn't get close enough to the glass. At least a dozen people had beaten him there.

Then, just 10 seconds after the first boom, there was a second blast. This one was truly massive. Some unknown *terrorist* had planted a huge bomb outside the building. The explosion was so powerful that it blew out windows a mile and a half away. People on the other side of town felt their buildings *shudder*. Nearby cars,

是1998年8月7日上午10:30。

盖塔拉·恩亚和别人一样好奇。这位48岁的废金属商人不在乌凡第大厦里工作。他碰巧到这里来看一个朋友。他也对听到的声音感到奇怪，他和其他人一起涌向窗户。恩亚尽量向外看，但是他无法靠近玻璃窗。他前面至少有12个人。

就在第一次爆炸发生10秒钟后，第二次爆炸发生了。这次是真格的了。不为人知的恐怖主义者在大楼外面安置了一个巨型炸弹。爆炸的威力把窗子炸到了一英里半的地方。小城另一边的人们都感到了他们的房子颤动。附近的轿车、卡车，甚至一辆公共汽车也起火了。

curious *adj.* 好奇的　　　　　　　　　　scurry *v.* 急赶；急跑
terrorist *n.* 恐怖主义者　　　　　　　　shudder *v.* 震动；颤动

trucks, and even a town bus *caught fire*.

It turned out that the real *target* of the terrorists was not the four-story Ufundi House. It was the American Embassy across the parking lot. But while the bomb did do great damage to the American Embassy, it totally flattened the smaller Ufundi House. In all, the blast killed 213 people. That made it one of the bloodiest terrorist acts ever. (The first blast turned out to be a grenade. Some people think it was used to draw workers to the windows in order to kill as many as possible with the bomb.)

In all, the blast injured almost 5,000 people, As grim as this toll was, though, it could have been even worse. Thanks to a group of brave rescue workers, some people buried in the *rubble* were saved. One was Gaitara Ng'ang'a.

"I was lucky," he said. "I was not hit directly." The people who

---

实际上恐怖主义分子的真实目标不是四层的乌凡第大楼，而是停车场对面的美国大使馆。这次爆炸也的确给美国大使馆造成了很大的破坏，但是它完全把小一点的乌凡第大楼炸毁了，总共伤亡213人。认为是最血腥的恐怖主义行动之一。（原来第一次爆炸是一个手榴弹，有些人认为它是用来把工作人员吸引到窗户前，以使第二次爆炸尽可能多地杀伤。）

这次爆炸大约伤及了5000人，实际上，情况甚至可能更糟。这完全要感谢一群勇敢的营救人员，使一些埋在废墟中的人得以获救，其中就有盖塔拉·恩亚。

"我很幸运，"他说，"我没有受到直接的伤害。"在他前面扑到窗

---

catch fire 着火

rubble *n.* 碎砖；瓦砾

target *n.* 目标

had rushed ahead of him to the windows took the full force of the blast and were killed. Ng'ang'a felt the building collapsing around him, burying him under a pile of concrete and steel. After the blast, he found himself trapped in a small clearing near some stairs. The space was just 4 feet high and 2 feet wide.

His left leg was broken and *pinned* under the rubble. Blood streaked down his face from deep cuts in his head, and some of his teeth were knocked out. Yet, *incredibly*, he stayed fairly calm. He recalled stories of people who had been trapped in collapsed buildings for days and were later saved. "I was expecting to wait two or three days," he said.

Ng'ang'a managed to reach into his pocket and *pull out* a *match*. Lighting it, he looked around. At the edge of the clearing where he sat there was a large hole. Even with a match, he couldn't see the

---

户前的人们完全受到了爆炸的冲击，全部死亡。恩亚感到大楼在他周围垮塌，把他埋在了一堆混凝土和钢筋的混合物中。爆炸后他发现他被困在一个不大的，靠近楼梯的小空隙中。这个空间有4英尺高，2英尺宽。

他的左腿骨折，被压在废墟中。鲜血从他头上很深的伤口流下，流到了脸上，他的一些牙齿被撞掉了。但是令人难以置信的是，他表现得相当冷静。他回忆起了那些被困在倒塌建筑废墟中几天，最终获救的人们。"我做了等待两到三天的准备，"他说。

恩亚竟吃力地在他的衣袋中取出火柴。点燃后，他向四周打量了一下。他坐着的地方旁边是一个大洞。即使是用火柴，也不能看到它的尽

---

pin *v.* 固定住；别住
pull out 取出

incredibly *adv.* 难以置信地
match *n.* 火柴

bottom. He had no idea how deep it was. He didn't want to find out the hard way. If the debris shifted, he might *slip into* the hole and fall so far that he would be killed. Ng'ang'a decided he had to get farther away from the hole, so he struggled to free his left leg. Using a *cable* wire that dangled overhead, he pulled himself up and away from the hole. Still, he was trapped under a mountain of debris. Sure that rescue workers were on the way, he fluffed up his coat into a pillow and went to sleep.

In fact, rescue workers had arrived on the scene. Soon they were sifting through the debris. But they had to work carefully. If they *disrupted* the balance of the rubble, the entire pile of steel and concrete could collapse. That would kill any survivors trapped underneath. "It is really a dicey operation trying to make sure nothing collapses on these people," said one of the rescuers.

头。他不知道它有多深。他也不想去看到底有多深。如果残骸发生移动，他有可能会滑进这个洞，可能会落得很深，要了他的命。恩亚决定离这个洞远点，所以他尽力挣脱左腿，他拉着头上悬挂的一段线缆，移动到了远离那个洞的地方。但是他还是在一堆废墟的底下。当然他也知道救援的活动正在展开，他把大衣拍成一个枕头，然后睡着了。

实际上救援人员已经到达了现场。很快他们开始小心仔细地搬运废墟。但是他们必须十分小心，因为如果他们破坏了整个废墟的平衡，整堆的钢筋和混凝土就会垮塌。那将会使里面埋着的幸存者丧生。"要保证一点也不倒塌，不伤及里面的幸存者真是很冒险，"一名救援者这样说。

---

slip into 滑入；滑进

disrupt *v.* 弄乱；扰乱

cable *n.* 电缆

Slowly, using tall *cranes*, they lifted *slabs* of concrete out of the way. They fired up *blowtorches* to cut steel rods. They used drills to slice through the smaller blocks of concrete. They also brought in specially trained dogs to locate some of the victims' bodies.

Meanwhile, rescuers kept calling out for anyone who was trapped. "Is anyone alive?" they shouted again and again. At last, the calls reached Ng'ang'a. By then he had been huddled in his little pitch-black space overnight. He had lost all sense of time. But he stirred himself and shouted out a *response*.

"Yes! Yes! Yes!" he yelled.

"What's your name?"

"Ng'ang'a!"

He kept hollering out his name. His calls helped rescuers determine exactly where he was. As they began digging down

---

人们使用高大的起重机把大块的混凝土板吊开。他们燃起喷灯切断钢筋，使用钻刀切开小的混凝土块。他们也带来了经过特殊训练的狗，来寻找遇难者。

当时，营救人员一直在呼唤那些被压在下面的人。"有没有活着的？"他们一次一次地喊。最后，喊声到达了恩亚。到那时为止，他已经在那个漆黑的小空间里面蜷缩了一夜，已经失去了时间观念。但是他强打起精神，喊话回答。

"有！有！有！"他大喊着。

"你叫什么名字？"

"恩亚！"

他不断地大喊着他的名字。他的呼救使救援人员能够确定他的位置。当

---

crane *n.* 起重机　　　　　　　　slab *n.* 厚板
blowtorch *n.* 喷灯　　　　　　　response *n.* 响应；反应；回答

toward him, Ng'ang'a was surprised to hear a female voice not far away. It belonged to a woman who was buried somewhere near him. "What did he say?" asked the woman.

"They are trying to save us," Ng'ang'a answered.

The woman said her name was Rose. Unlike Ng'ang'a, she was *panicky*. Her face was badly burned and she felt very *thirsty*. She desperately wanted to get out as fast as possible. She even asked Ng'ang'a if she could be rescued first.

But he had no control over that. Although Rose was near him, she was trapped in a place that was much more difficult to reach. As rescuers dug closer to Ng'ang'a, he tried to *reassure* Rose. "If I go," he said, "they will come next for you."

Then, at last, the *rescuers* broke through to Ng'ang'a. They could not pull him out right away. It took more hours of drilling and digging

---

人们开始向他挖掘时，恩亚奇怪地听到离他不远处有一个女性的声音。那是在他附近某处被压住的一名女子的声音。"他说什么？"那个女人问。

"他们正在试图救我们，"恩亚回答道。

女人的名字叫罗斯。不像恩亚，她显得惊慌失措，脸上有很严重的烧伤，她觉得很渴。所以急切地想出去。她甚至问恩亚她能否先得到营救。

但是他并不能控制这一点。虽然罗斯离他很近，但是她被困的地点更难于到达。随着营救者挖掘接近了恩亚，他试图对罗斯进行保证。"如果我被救走了，"他说，"他们马上就会来救你。"

最后，救援人员到达了恩亚的面前。他们不能马上把他拉出来，又花

---

panicky *adj.* 恐慌的   thirsty *adj.* 口渴的
reassure *v.* 使……安心；恢复某人的信心   rescuer *n.* 救助者

to free him. But at last, 36 hours after the blast, they *lifted* him out of the rubble.

The rescuers then went after Rose. They tried frantically to reach her in time. "I just told her to hold on, we're coming for her," said Bob Nasser, a Kenyan rescue worker. For a while, Rose answered him. "Yes," she kept saying. But rescuers could tell from her voice that she was very weak.

The last time anyone heard Rose speak was at 3 P.M. on Sunday afternoon. "Since then, we've heard nothing," said a Red Cross worker. "There's just no sound coming back."

Sadly, Rose did not *survive* long enough to be rescued. For Gaitara Ng'ang'a, the Nairobi bombing had been a close call. But for Rose and 212 other victims, it brought *untimely* death.

了几个小时又钻又挖才把他救出来。最后，在爆炸发生36小时后，他们把他从废墟中挖了出来。

营救人员马上搜索罗斯。他们疯狂地想尽快到达她的面前。"我告诉她要坚持住，我们就来营救她，"鲍勃·纳塞，一名肯尼亚救援者说。曾经有一段时间，罗斯回答他："可以，"她一直在说。但是救援人员从声音能够听出来她十分虚弱。

我们最后听到罗斯的说话声是在星期日下午的3点钟。"从那以后，我们什么也没有听见，"一位红十字的人员说，"就是没有回答的声音。"

可悲的是，罗斯没有活得足够长等来救援。对于盖塔拉·恩亚来说这次内罗毕爆炸事件是一次紧急情况。但是对于罗斯和其他212名遇难者来说，它带来的是过早的死亡。

---

lift *v.* 挖出；抬起   survive *v.* 幸存
untimely *adj.* 过早的；不合时宜的